Lessons from Carrying the Tortoise

Lessons from Carrying the Tortoise

Unique True Stories and Lessons of a Christian Life

Kit Nongkhlaw

RESOURCE *Publications* · Eugene, Oregon

LESSONS FROM CARRYING THE TORTOISE
Unique True Stories and Lessons of a Christian Life

Resource Publications
An Imprint of Wipf and Stock Publishers
199 W. 8th Ave., Suite 3
Eugene, OR 97401

www.wipfandstock.com

PAPERBACK ISBN: 979-8-3852-2633-7
HARDCOVER ISBN: 979-8-3852-2634-4
EBOOK ISBN: 979-8-3852-2635-1

VERSION NUMBER 08/21/24

Dedicated to my Parents

Contents

CONTENTS

Preface

THERE ARE COUNTLESS BOOKS on Christian faith, Christian lessons, and Christian life experiences written from the Western or Developed World perspectives.

However, I have written this book, "Lessons from Carrying the Tortoise, Unique True Stories and Lessons of a Christian life," from a different perspective. I want to present to the world these true stories written from the Third or Developing World perspectives.

These true stories are about the life of a Tribal Christian from North East India, growing up in a poor yet devout Christian family.

In this life, we encounter many unique, beautiful and exotic things. Parents, siblings, mother-nature, animals (wild and tamed), people and countless other things can change and mold our lives if we take the time to observe and learn.

Inside these true stories, there are miracles, hidden gems and unique lessons in life. These stories taught me to have a meaningful Christian life while traversing the ever challenging life's valley of sorrow and joy.

We live in a modern world of make-belief but the stories inside these pages are genuine. I believe the lessons from these stories are universal despite being unique.

Life is beautiful if we take the time to learn from its lessons. This book tells us these unique life changing lessons and many more.

Scriptures taken from the New King James Version. Copyright © 1982 by Thomas Nelson, Inc. Used by permission. All rights reserved.

Preface

The events written in this book are not chronological in order.

I am grateful to Kyle Lundburg for designing the covers and Matt Wimer, Managing Editor, Wipf and Stock Publishers for helping and guiding me to make this book as it is.

26th May 2024   Kit Nongkhlaw

PART I

Lessons of Life in Ageville

1

Going to Church but on Wrong Days

THERE WAS THIS WOMAN who went to church to worship God, sometimes on a Saturday, sometimes on a Sunday and sometimes on a Monday. How and why?

This is the story our father told us when we asked him how he went and taught in his third mission morning school.

Ageville[1] is a small remote village surrounded to the east by the beautiful plateau of cliffs and hills. To the north, west and south are the fertile lands of small hills and valleys. It was initially a tiny hamlet.

However, all the vacant lands are community lands. Anybody can take any vacant land and use it as much as you can. As long as you use the land, it is yours, but if you abandon it for three consecutive years, anybody can take over and use it.

There are a few villagers who have settled here since time immemorial. However, after World War II, people from hilly areas flocked to this tiny hamlet to get the free land available.

Gradually, the hamlet grew to a small village. However, most of the villagers here were illiterate. There are many stories about the people who settled here. Some of them are tragic and others are funny or success stories.

There was one old woman who came and make this village her home. She was from a small village near Rabja, where our father was a mission

1. Name changed

3

morning school teacher for some years. Her life was tragic. She married the love of her life. She gave birth to many children, but all of them died after birth or when they were small children.

But the most tragic part was that her husband also died leaving her alone. She lived a bitter and lonely life. All avoided or looked down at her. She was an outcast in society.

Then she came to know about Jesus, the friend of the outcasts and the downtrodden. When she learned about Jesus' love and salvation, she accepted Him as her Lord and Savior.

But her problems increased after she became a Christian. Her close relatives, who were non-Christians, disowned her. They excommunicated her from the clan. She was no longer welcome to family rituals or gatherings. And none of her relatives would enter her house.

Then she came to know about the new village, Ageville. You can get land as much as you can use and all are free. People talked of many opportunities in this new village. On hearing about this, this middle-aged woman left her village to live in Ageville.

This woman sold everything she had in her old village. She left everything, her friends, relatives, and the old way of life. She looked forward to a new life in this new village and being free to worship her Lord.

When she landed at Ageville, other villagers helped her. They helped her choose a vacant land on the slope of one beautiful small hill to the north of the village. There, on top of the hill, the villagers helped her construct a beautiful thatched-roof hut. She made this place her new home.

To help her loneliness, she adopted two dogs as her companions. Then she built a chicken coop and kept plenty of local chickens. Later, she built a pigsty and kept a few pigs. She planted various types of vegetables. The woman planted various tropical fruits in her garden.

She planted rice in the flat land below her hut. She lived a lonely but happy life. Her close friends were the pet animals she kept. She was always so busy on her farm that she had no time to worry.

When the village grew, they built a small thatched-roof church. The Christian community in the village was happy to get a church. They started gathering for Sunday worship service.

A few weeks later, all was well. All the Christians there went to church on the right day, on Sunday, except one person. That exception was this woman from nearby Rabja.

This woman could not read or write. She was unsure about which day was a Sunday. Sometimes, she would come to church on Sunday, sometimes on Monday, and sometimes on Saturday. How come?

Before the coming of the Missionaries, the people here had an eight days week. They have a market on each day of the week in different places of bigger villages. They gave the name of the day as per the village or the place they held the market.

This woman could count these market days, but since it was an eight days week, she was confused. Therefore, many times she would go to church on Saturday or Monday instead of Sunday.

When she went to church on Saturday or Monday and found nobody there, she would go to her friends' houses. There, they would tell her it was Saturday or Monday. After a few mistakes like this, she thought she would change her strategy. She would not count her days on market days, but with an alternative approach.

Then she thought of a new novel idea. She had egg-laying hens. She took one hen and the place it used to lay its eggs. Every evening, she would check the eggs. She started counting them from Monday onwards. If there were six eggs, then she would go to church on the next day.

But one day she found she went to church on Monday. Why? Because the particular hen did not lay an egg for one day. The hen had a gap in her egg-laying process. She tried a few weeks, but it did not work out well. Frequently, she went on the right Sunday, but then she made mistakes again.

However, the old woman would not quit her efforts. Somebody told her to put separately a grain of rice each day she cooked. She tried this. But again, there was a problem. The grain of rice was too small and therefore, it was difficult for her to count. Sometimes she lost the place she kept these grains of rice.

As the grain of rice was too small and problematic for her to count, she tried another method. Every morning when she woke up and lit a fire in her fire-place, she would put aside one piece of firewood. It worked for a few weeks but again, now this woman had become older and occasionally she would forget to put aside the piece of firewood. Then again, she would go to church on the wrong day.

The entire village knew about the story of this old woman. The Christians of the village held a meeting to solve this problem. They discussed the problem of this old woman. When they debated about this issue, then came the discussion about their children. One day, their children would be like this old woman because of a lack of education.

They needed to do something. To solve this problem, they needed a school. Not for this old woman, but for the future of their children. Finally, they decided the village needed a school.

Therefore, they approached the mother church where most of the village Christians came from. The church agreed to their request. This church knew that our father had resigned from his job as a teacher in Rabja. They approached him to come and start a school here in Ageville.

When our father consulted our mother, they agreed that this was a call for them. So, our father agreed to come and start a new school, a third one, in this small, beautiful village.

At first, he went there only by himself, leaving us at our grandmother's house. They renovated the small thatched roof church and made it bigger so that they could use it as a school on weekdays and a church on Sundays.

When he knew about the story of this woman, our father built his thatched-roof house on a flat hillock near to this old woman. He intended to teach her and also would go to her house every Sunday to take her to the church.

Therefore, apart from his school duty, our father went and taught this old woman how to count. He started teaching her, with the help of small stones, how to add and subtract. This woman was a good learner. The problem with her was that nobody had ever explained or taught her.

After learning how to count, she wanted to know how to read. She wanted to read because she wanted to sing hymns in the church. Slowly and gradually, with the teaching of our father, this woman could sing some of the common hymns used in the church.

Finally, there was no more problem. This woman was astute in keeping her accounts of days and money. She would use Saturday to wash herself and her clothes and Sunday to attend church. There were no more mistakes. But most important was that now, she could sing songs of praise to the Lord.

When people attend this small village church, they would see the radiant face of this old woman. Once an outcast, she found acceptance here. She was once lonely, but now she had many friends. This old woman was once looked down on by her relatives, but now people respect her for what she is. She was once illiterate, but now she could count, read and she could sing songs of praise.

She is now the happiest woman because she can worship God freely.

From loneliness to happiness,

From poverty to self-sufficiency,

From down-trodden to contentment,
From hatred and regret, to forgive and forget,
From a life of longings to a life of blessings,
From a life of nothing to a life of meaning,
God has given me everything.
Then our father concluded, saying,

"Sons, there are many lessons from the life of this godly woman. The core lesson is to persist and never quit. Persistence is key. Keep trying if you don't succeed.

The next important lesson is life is full of trials and difficulties. No one is free from these problems of life. All have to go through such problems and difficulties. However, serving the Lord brings true and everlasting peace.

Finally, I want to tell you that education is extremely important in life. I have seen with my own eyes how education changes people's lives. Embrace knowledge and education in your life."

I knew it was by the grace and guidance of God, our father got to teach in this small remote village. I firmly believed God had a plan for our family, especially for me, because our stay in this remote village taught us countless unique life lessons and changed our lives forever.

2

The Bull Owner—I

THE ENEMY LAID A *trap by asking to say just a few words. Because of these few words by the wife, the husband had to pay a fine equivalent to more than one year of his salary. Could this break the family? Or could it make them more united?*

We have a sizable garden where our parents planted many things. Besides the tropical fruits all around the garden, they planted corn, yams, and sweet potatoes. They also grow various types of vegetables, like pumpkins, cucumbers, beans, and other local exotic vegetables.

Our mother was the key person looking after the garden. Our father would help her with ploughing, planting, and other major works. However, taking care of these plants and vegetables like weeding, watering, pruning was the responsibility of our mother.

We enjoyed accompanying our mother to this garden. She would allow us to help her, like watering and plugging the weeds. She would gently touch the plants wherever she could. When we asked her why she did this, she answered that plants and vegetables, like children, feel happy and important when we touch them with love.

Therefore, our mother took great care of her garden the way she cared for us. Because of her special care and attention, all that she planted grew well. This garden supplied us with all that we needed as a family.

Our father also worked hard to make this garden beautiful. He dug the ditch all around the garden. On top of the ditch, he built the exquisite bamboo picket fence to protect animals from entering this beautiful garden.

Then one day, a big bull somehow destroyed the fence and entered the garden to trample, eat, and destroy the plants and vegetables. This bull destroyed the beautiful fence and also the plants and vegetables. Nobody saw how the bull entered the garden.

When our dogs barked so fiercely, our mother went out to investigate. She saw the big bull trampling over and eating her plants and vegetables. She ran out to the garden. While running, she found a large enough stick. With this stick, she chased and hit the bull. She cried when she saw the destruction of her well-maintained garden.

Down below from our garden, there was a ditch made by our father as part of the boundary of our land. While our mother chased this bull, it fell into this ditch. The bull tried to get out of the ditch but could not. In the meantime, it did more harm to itself.

The bull owner was hiding somewhere behind the bush when this happened. He was watching how things would work out. When he saw this, he came out from hiding. Later, as pre-planned, his cronies came to witness the incident.

There were heated arguments between them and our mother. Under duress, our mother had to bend to their pressure by massaging this bull in the ditch and said these words,

"I am sorry I chased and hit you."

The bull owner wanted her to massage the bull and to speak these words. This was what they wanted from her. With no hint of the danger, she innocently walked straight into the trap the owner of the bull had set for her.

Later that evening, many villagers came to see the bull trapped inside the ditch. They tried to pull the bull from the ditch. The bull had broken its legs and injured itself. With great difficulty, they could pull this bull, but sadly, it could no longer walk.

In this part of the world and in those days, the bull was an extremely important animal. Any household that had a bull, or especially two bulls, was rich. A pair of bulls were used to plough the field or paddy fields. They were also used to extract logs from the forest.

An injured bull was no longer useful to them. The only utility was to kill it and eat its meat. To add more miseries to our parents, the bull later died on the spot near the ditch. Once it died, nobody would eat its meat. The only way was to bury the bull. But that was not the end. There were more problems ahead.

The bull owner insisted they should hold a village council or durbar to determine the punishment or fine for the death of the bull. The bull owner refused to settle the issue amicably, but wanted an impossibly exorbitant fine from our parents.

Now, our parents understood it was a trap. The owner of the bull wanted to extort money from them. He wanted them to pay an extremely heavy price. They were not sure about the actual reasons, but they could guess.

The bull owner was the previous headman of Ageville. He held this post for quite a long time. They voted him out in the recent village council because of multiple reasons. The entire village elected our father to be their new headman. The bull owner could not accept his defeat and planned revenge for our father.

When they understood the reason, they agreed to take the matter to the traditional village council/ durbar. They wanted the matter to be decided once and for all. Once they took the matter to the village council, everything would become clear. The only problem was that our father was the newly elected headman. As a headman, he had to take the final decision.

They convened the durbar or village council. All the grown-up men attended the durbar. In those days, they did not allow the women inside the durbar. The village durbar ground was full. Those from the side of the bull owner came fully prepared. They wanted to know what the new headman would do in this circumstance.

As the case involved our father, the incumbent headman, he volunteered to step down. However, the village durbar would not let him do that. They forced him to chair the durbar and make the final decision.

Witnesses came and testified. Both sides made heated arguments. Those who were from our parents' side blamed the bull owner for allowing the bull to enter the fenced garden. But no one saw it happen.

The bull owner's side said that the bull would have been ok, but it died because our mother massaged it and said, 'sorry'. They dwelt on the massaging and the word sorry.

Our mother was guilty, otherwise, why would she massage and say 'sorry'? When you use the word sorry, it means you accepted you were wrong. That was the traditional way and belief.

Our father, as a headman, handled the welfare of the village. The bull owner claimed that when he was a headman, nothing of the sort happened. Now that the village elected a new headman, problems cropped up in the village.

And since the wife of the headman was involved and held guilty, they blamed the entire family for being responsible. They demanded a fine double the cost of the live bull and equivalent to more than one year's salary of our father.

There was chaos in the durbar. It almost came to a fistfight. Our father had to calm down both sides. He saw that an amicable settlement was impossible.

Revenge would not settle. When a man wanted revenge, he could go to any length. In some other villages, there were arson, destroying of crops, the burning of houses, and even murder because of such issues.

During the arguments, our father kept his calm. He heard a deep, silent voice in his heart to settle the issue. Then, our father raised his hand to silence the durbar. With deep solemnity, he said,

"For the sake of the village, the welfare of the society we lived in, and to solve the problem forever, I and my family will pay the fine."

The whole durbar was silent. You could hear the pin drop. The bull owner and his cronies were stunned. Nobody in the village could pay such a huge amount of fine except our parents.

As a young child, I was also stunned when we discussed this story at home. I asked our father why he did that?

Our father answered,

"Son, there are many things in life which we have to do and learn our lessons.

First, no matter how strong the fence you built or beautiful your garden, there would always be a bull owner who would let lose his bull to spoil that garden. That is the way of human nature and human hearts.

Second, your mother is a strong woman for having the courage to say sorry. She grew up with Christian principles guiding her. In traditional belief, saying sorry is a sign of weakness, but to us, it is a sign of humility and courage. In your life, be humble and have the courage to say sorry whenever needed."

I looked at our mother with admiration. Any other husband would have blamed her for being foolish. Any other wife would have blamed her husband for taking the job of the headman and brought such misery to the family. There would be no end to the quarrels. But our parents loved each other and understood each other well.

If they blame each other, there would be no peace in the family. So, our father continued,

"Third, the bull owner had set his mind to revenge and extorted money from us. The election of a new headman was something he couldn't tolerate. That was clear, as we shall see. He could have done worse than what he did. By doing good things to your enemy, it will be a blessing for us.

Fourth, the entire village would have split into two factions. That won't do us any good. There would be enmity and hatred. As a Christian, a schoolteacher, and a headman, I cannot let that happen.

Fifth, if I refused to pay the fine, there would be more problems. There would be no peace for both sides. Hatred begat hatred and there will be no end to it.

There are many more lessons, but at least I want to say this. I heard the deep, silent voice in my heart. The voice, which I believe is from God, told me to be humble and do good things to your enemy.

The bull owner had set his mind to revenge and extorted money from us as a family. But by doing this, he sets out to revenge himself and his family. The feeling of seeking revenge will eat his heart and destroy his peace of mind. He hoped that money would destroy or make us poorer, but in fact, it would strengthen our family.

He got his money and the temporary feeling of being powerful. But these are temporary and will never last. In the end, he will regret what he did. But for us, we have love, integrity, trust, faith, unity, and hope, which will last forever."

I thank God that our parents not only taught us about God and Christian principles, but they lived by those principles. They instilled in our young minds those higher valuable godly things in life which we should pursue rather than temporal things like money and fame.

3

The Bull Owner—II

By utilising and twisting words, he trapped her. She would also trap and defeat him with patience and by cleverly using words.

We never doubted the words of our father. Therefore, let us find out the results of this unusual fight between the bull owner and our parents.

To promise to pay the fine was okay, but to part with the money was a challenge. However, to our parents, words once uttered, a promise made, and integrity were more important than money. So, in front of the witnesses, our father paid the fine to the bull owner.

Upon receiving the money, the bull owner did as expected. This was easy money he got and therefore it was also easy money to spend.

A few days later, he prepared an extravagant feast. He invited all his cronies to the feast. He also ordered an enormous quantity of country made liquor.

At the feast that night, alcohol poured freely while they discussed the trap the bull owner laid out for our parents. The bull owner told his cronies everything.

How it hurt his pride when he lost the election for the post of village headman. He told them in detail of how he devised a plan to ruin the newly elected headman and his family.

As a traditional believer, he knew the power of words. With words, you could do almost anything. There was a belief that even stones obeyed humans with the proper use of words. They did that when they erected gigantic monoliths. They could pull the monolith to the place they wanted by using words with the pumpkin straws as ropes.

Therefore, to trap the schoolteacher directly would be difficult. He used his ingenuity by trapping his simple wife. He carefully planned and laid the trap for her when the husband was away.

The bull owner stealthily destroyed the bamboo fencing to allow his hungry bull to enter inside the garden. Once inside the garden, the bull would trample and eat the plants and vegetables. He knew the wife would chase the bull. He knew there was a ditch where he expected the bull could fall.

After he pushed the bull inside, he observed everything from his hiding place while his cronies were waiting nearby to act as witnesses. While he proudly narrated the traps he made, he told his cronies to keep the secret.

The only problem with the secret was that walls have ears. In a small village, drunks could never keep the secrets. This secret became an open secret.

From one mouth, it went to another mouth. From one ear, it went to another ear. And then it came to our parents' ears. The trusted friends of our parents came and told our parents what they knew.

Some of the old folks came and cautioned our parents. They stressed on the power and importance of words. They told our parents that when dealing with traditional believers, to be mindful of the words they use. Therefore, their advice was to use words wisely.

When our parents knew about this trap, anger filled their hearts but kept their cool. They knew they would not get back their money. However, they devised a strategy which they thought would work.

They prayed to God, asking for wisdom on how to deal with the matter. Patience would be their best strategy. As a result, they were patient enough to wait. Someday, the bull owner could make a mistake or a wrong move.

They decided our father would do nothing. A man fighting another man would be dangerous. However, with a woman, it would be a different matter. The bull owner trapped our mother with words and she will trap and defeat him with words.

A few months passed. When the bull owner saw our parents did nothing, he showed his true colors. Inside his heart, he was full of pride, power, and arrogance. Everywhere he went, he boasted about his invincibility.

Then, one fine day, the bull owner and two of his cronies were walking to cross the small village river. They saw our mother washing clothes at the river downstream. She was alone with nobody there.

With his conceit and pride, the bull owner took this opportunity to humiliate her. Along with his cronies, they came near to where she was washing the clothes. The bull owner started humiliating her with improper words mixed with sexual innuendo.

Our mother prepared herself for this time. She prayed a silent prayer to God for the courage and wisdom on how to use the words.

Before she said anything, she took a big enough stone from the river to protect herself for any eventuality. In her mind, she had already chosen the words to use. Then she forcefully said,

"We knew everything about your plans to trap me and my family. You extorted money from us by using your dirty tricks. We are Christians, and that's why we paid you. We thought the matter was closed.

However, it appears you wanted more. But by wanting more, you would lose all. Revenge will never work, because revenge will one day come back to you."

Then, with forceful feminine power, she spat and burst out,

"With such behaviour and words you used at me as a woman, I can never treat you as a human being, but a beast.

With such words, you don't deserve to wear a man's clothes but a woman's clothing. Come near me and I will make you wear these women's clothes.

I dare you to touch me. I have these women's clothes and I'll make you wear them. When I make you wear women's clothing, you will no longer be a man."

While holding the stone in her hand, with malice, she spitefully said,

"Come and lay your hands on me and I will destroy your manliness forever. However, if you are a cheap sissy woman, go away. And if you go away, you will be a weak, unworthy woman forever."

These words stunned the bull owner. If he approached her, he knew what the angry woman would do. She would hurl the stone at him. The force of that stone would surely destroy his manliness or might kill him. And to flee away was to accept defeat.

The bull owner's cronies were too shocked to take any action. The bull owner was their leader. They were waiting for him to tell them what to do. They just follow orders.

As luck would have it, they saw some people coming. It was evening and farmers were returning home.

The bull owner and his cronies then fled. They knew our mother would blame them for their indecent behaviour. They knew what would happen if our mother took the matter to the village durbar.

They knew the consequences of such an action. It was a village, and a traditional sacred code of behaviour applies to everybody. No man uses sexual innuendo and misbehaves with a woman.

A few days later, words spread like wildfire that our mother called the bull owner, a cheap sissy woman. The entire village knew about the encounter between the bull owner and our mother at the river. His cronies were the witnesses.

For a man to be called a woman was the curse to the traditional believer. And then to be spitted upon by a woman, that too in front of witnesses, that's the worst any man could take.

In this part of the world and the community we lived, a man is a man. Respect and decorum were part and parcel of village life. Therefore, nobody called a man a sissy or a cheap woman. And the worst part, nobody ever threatened to destroy his manliness.

The bull owner could not digest the words our mother hurled at him. To him, the words our mother used and shouted were a curse. He had no words or ideas to counter this curse.

Days and nights, these words our mother shouted at him rang in his ears. He believed his plan had succeeded, and he was the winner. But now he was a loser, and he was losing big time. If he lost the fight to a man, somehow he could take it. But to lose to a woman, it was beyond him.

Slowly, the bull owner started losing things. He lost his health, his money, and his friends. But the most important thing he lost was his self-respect. The entire village looked down at him.

Whatever he did, it was unsuccessful. His cattle died one by one from unknown causes. Locusts, rats, or wild animals destroyed his crops. He burned charcoal, but they all became ashes. He was now a sick pauper with only skin and bones.

The family quarrelled daily. There was no more peace for him and the family. He became a drunkard. The family was on the verge of begging for food, which hardly happened in the village.

Unable to bear the shame and the heavy burden of his heart, at last, he left the village. He and his family left empty-handed. According to some reports, he went and stayed in an unknown village far away.

From this story, we learnt many lessons and deeper things in life. Some of these are:

Pride goes before destruction.

It is better to give than to receive.

Words have power, use words wisely.

Walls have ears.

You reap what you sow.

Patience is bitter but its fruits are sweet.

If you dig the grave for others—you will fall there yourself.

Excessive liquor will bring your downfall.

The heavy burden of a guilty conscience; and many more.

Were our parents happy when these bad things happened to the bull owner? No. The most surprising lesson for us was that our parents, as Christians, prayed for him and his family. They prayed that one day he would realize his mistakes and change.

4

Catching Fishes with the Kettle

OPPORTUNITIES, BIG AND SMALL, *are everywhere. Could we see and find those opportunities in unlikely places?*

Our father had built a beautiful thatched roof house in Ageville, large enough for us to live and stay. When everything was ready, he came to fetch us from our grandmother's house and took us to live there. There are many wonderful stories about our lives there, the unique lessons we learnt and this is one of the earliest ones.

To the southeast of our thatched-roof house, there is a small, beautiful river. The source of this river is from the hills to the east of the village. Paddy fields dotted the slopes on both sides of this enchanting small river. It is also the major water source for pets and wild animals. Along the banks, there are various types of wild tropical fruits, some poisonous and some edible.

As long as this river flows, I will remember its clear turquoise water and its golden sandy beaches. Along the river, there are plenty of natural rocks and stones made beautiful by the erosion of millions of years. A few rocks protruded from the middle of the river withstanding the force of the current during the monsoon flood.

A little ahead, there is a small waterfall. The sound from this waterfall makes a beautiful chorus so smooth and calming to the ears. There are plenty of fishes, big and small. We can see the fishes swimming with glee in the clear turquoise water.

Every Saturday, our mother went to this river to wash clothes. She would always take us, me and my brother, along with her. Every Saturday, we looked forward to this ritual as we got to play in the water and enjoyed our childish creativity. The sand, the pebbles, the stones, the trees, and mostly the water were the ideal things to make our day.

While our mother was busy cleaning and washing, our world was brimming with joy and happiness. While playing with my brother near the river, we saw tiny small fishes swim freely in the clear turquoise water.

Oh, how could we catch them? We tried with our bare hands, but these small tiny fishes were too smart for us. They were almost in our hands when they freed themselves. This made us more determined to catch them. There should be a way to catch them.

In our childish adventure, we tried our best to catch these fishes. Then I saw the kettle which we brought from home to clean it and to carry the water back home. Then a thought came to my mind: we could use this kettle to catch fishes.

We took the kettle and put it in the water and watched for the fishes to enter inside the kettle. My brother and I remained silent to avoid disturbing the fishes.

The moment the fishes accidentally entered the kettle, we pulled up the kettle. We took the kettle and poured down the water in the sand along the river bank. The sand sucked the water, leaving the fishes jumping on the sand. But with this process, there were problems.

If we kept the handle of the kettle in our hands, the fishes would not enter inside. If we left the kettle with the handle, the water was a little deep and by the time we took the handle; the fishes had gotten out of the kettle. A few fishes came and entered the kettle without baits. We have to find a better way to catch these fishes.

Then we saw that in the nearby jungle, there were creeper plants. So, we cut the creeper plants with sharp rocks, tied them to the handle of the kettle, and watched from a little farther. That way, the fishes would not know us and would enter the kettle. When we saw the fishes enter the kettle, we pulled it fast enough that the fishes would not have time to get out.

So, every Saturday, we would gladly take the kettle, then some portion of leftover cooked rice as bait for our fish-catching adventure. Our mother allowed us to do so because she would be free to carry on her cleaning and washing. Meanwhile, we were close to her and she could see us.

The moment we reached the river, both my brother and I put some pieces of cooked rice as bait inside the kettle. We cut the creeper plant with sharp rocks and tied it in the kettle's handle. We then put the kettle at the bottom of the river, changing the spot now and then.

From a little distance, we observed the small fishes enter the kettle. Once we saw that a few fishes entered, we pulled the kettle as fast as we could through the creeper plant. Then we took the kettle to the sand and poured out the water. The small fishes jumped and struggled themselves in the sand. We caught these fishes covered with sand and kept them separately in a pot with some water.

By the time our mother finished her washing and cleaning, we would have catch plenty of small fishes. In one day, we could catch hundreds of these fishes. When we left the river, we carried the pot carefully and proudly showed our father our day's catches.

Every week, our parents made different recipes for these fishes. Sometimes, they added vegetable(s) to match with the fishes. Then they would also put the fishes inside the banana leaf, folded it carefully. Then they put it inside the clay oven covered with hot ashes and live charcoal.

From experience, they knew when the fishes was ready. Then they removed the folded banana leaf from the fire, and mixed the fishes with onion and ginger. The taste was always too good to explain.

These were small things indeed in our childhood day-to-day life. However, when I look back now, I see these things differently. They were small things but always full of meanings. These are some of life's lessons we learned from these small things:

First, creativity. We used whatever things were available to create something creative. With whatever tools we have, we use these things to have fun and enjoy ourselves. We did not have artificial toys, but we made creative toys from things available with nature.

Second, time management. Our mother could concentrate on her work without distraction from us. We never waste time, but use it for something useful and productive. We also have to know the exact time to take out the kettle from the water.

Third, patience. To wait for the fishes to enter the kettle required patience. Wait and wait and be vigilant. We never knew at what time these fishes would enter the kettle. By doing this the whole day, it helped to build up our patience.

Fourth, concentration. We have to concentrate on seeing how many fishes have entered the kettle. With concentration, we knew exactly at what time to pull out the kettle. Once we put the kettle in the water, we have to focus and be attentive.

Fifth, timing and speed. We need to pull the kettle from the water at the correct time and right speed. If we were too slow, the fishes would get out of the kettle.

Sixth, a drop makes an ocean. Sometimes, only one or two fishes entered the kettle. However, by evening, we had caught hundreds of them. We learned to value small things because out of these small things that big things were possible.

Seven, having fun. Some children had no fun. But for us, standing in the cool water, seeing the fishes enter the kettle, pulling out the kettle, and then seeing the fishes struggling in the sand was fun. Then catching those small fishes with our bare hands was an experience that few children would get.

Eight, reward and profit. When we reached home and showed the fishes to our father was what we looked forward to. The smiles on the face of our parents made our day. Not only that, but we could contribute something to the family even when that contribution was tiny.

Ninth, make our parents happy. As children, we wanted to make our parents happy. To see their smiling faces, to hear their appreciation and the happiness we created, was beyond description.

Tenth, competitive spirit. I competed with my younger brother when we caught those fishes jumping and struggling in the sand. When my brother could catch more fishes than me, I felt ashamed that he could do better than me. But my younger brother was equally good or sometimes better than me.

Eleventh, in tune with nature. We got to play in the clear river water, which flowed slowly under our feet was a genuine joy. To learn how to swim by the trial-and-error method in the clear shallow water, I think few could get. Then the delight when we could float in the water.

Twelfth, happy childhood. There were many problems in life because of child abuse and many other problems. We were so fortunate to have a blessed childhood. I am what I am today because of all these small but precious experiences.

These are only a few life lessons we learnt in this small beautiful remote village but there are many more. It is difficult to name them all, like those small rocks protruding in the river withstanding the force of nature and many more but suffice to say that it is an experience beyond words to live in tune with nature.

Through these experiences, God had prepared elaborate plans for me and my brother. Because through these small insignificant things, we learned valuable lessons in life and could navigate through various tapestries and problems of life.

But most important is the sense of wonder in God's creation and the belief in His wonderful power. These small experiences, though insignificant, strengthen my faith in God. Because those peals of laughter, thrills, joys, and happiness of those childhood days gone by will remain with me forever.

5

The Dogs Saved Us

SHORT-SIGHTEDNESS BROUGHT MANY MISERIES. Farsightedness brought joy, progress, and security.

One day, our father brought to our house two small cute local pups, a male, and a female. We were happy to have these pups with us, while our mother was not that happy.

To us, as children, the pups were so cute and lovely, while to our mother, the problems would be the hygiene and cleanliness from their urination and poops.

That night, after dinner, we discussed the pups. To us, they were the most valuable pets we could be friends and play. To our mother, it would be a problem to take care of their poops.

But to our father, it was a long-term investment, benefit and security. Regarding the hygiene and cleanliness, he told our mother he would take care and train them where to urinate and poop.

Then our father explained to us the benefits of having pups. It would help us young children to learn how to take care of pets. He entrusted us with the responsibility of feeding them. Dogs, known as humans' best friends, would also provide us with companionship and playmates.

However, the most important thing was that we stayed on a hilltop a little far away from our nearest neighbors. Our house was a thatch hut constructed with small timbers and bamboo. Anybody could break in and enter inside. The dogs would be our security and guard us for any eventuality.

After our father explained all these details, our mother hesitantly accepted the pups. Then one thing remained: their names. Our father challenged us to make interesting names for these pups. It was fun to suggest names for these small pups.

At last we settled for Thohmut—(Stripes-nose) stripes around the nose for the male, and Thohmat—(Stripes-eyes) stripes near the eyes for the female pup. Therefore, from that evening onwards, these were the names of these two pups.

We had the best times looking and caring for these pups. Our father trained them so well that they never pooped or urinated near the house, but a little farther away in a particular place outside and behind our house. We saw with our own eyes how our father trained these small pups. They were so disciplined once we trained them.

Our father continued as a mission school teacher at Ageville. His salary was meagre. At today's rate, his salary per month would be around half a dollar, but in those days, it might be worth more.

Therefore, to support his family, he worked in his fields and tried his hands at various trades. Meanwhile, these two local pups grew up to mature dogs.

Later, our father came in contact with one timber merchant. This timber merchant paid the forest owners and then cut the timbers for sale. He had many people employed and worked under him. All his workers and laborers were illiterate. He needed someone educated enough to look after his work as a manager.

When he came to know about our father, he offered him the job of a manager. Our father accepted the offer, as this would mean an extra income for him. So, almost every day, he would go to his work after school and come back home in the evening.

Because our father was honest and good at his job, the merchant's timber business grew. The works of felling timbers stretched out and went farther and farther away. Our father tried his best to make sure he didn't stay overnight anywhere that would create a conflict with his position as a morning schoolteacher.

One day, he found himself with important work to do at the school and also at home. He could not go at his usual time to oversee the felling and accounting of timbers.

Therefore, he had to leave for his work for the timber merchant late in the afternoon. He told us he would try to come back home if possible, but otherwise, he might stay over and come home early the next morning for his school duties.

While walking to the place of work, he met a stranger on the way. They talked to each other. This stranger asked our father where he would go so late in the afternoon. With no suspicion at all, as our father was a good man, he told this stranger that he was going to his work as a manager a little farther away.

This stranger enquired whether he could come back home, as it was already evening. Our father replied he would look at the situation, and if required, he could stay back. They said their goodbyes and went in different directions.

Later during that night, the barking of Thohmut and Thohmat, the two dogs, jolted our mother from sleep. She knew there was someone out there with malicious intentions. The dogs were barking in a threatening and loud manner, preventing the unknown person from entering the compound.

Our mother now realized the dangers we were in. We were sleeping peacefully, unaware that the danger was lurking outside. Here is the contrast of young children with grown-ups. The children have no concerns because they knew their parents would protect them. The grown-ups fought strange but tough fights to protect their children.

Our mother was determined, no matter what, to protect herself and her two children. Therefore, she went to the kitchen and took the machete.

She sat on the edge of the bed where we slept while she kept the machete handy. She looked upon us, two tiny, powerless children, and the sight of their innocence brought tears to her eyes. We were sleeping peacefully, unaware of the dangers. She looked at us with a tender heart and love.

When our mother told us this story, I imagined her dilemma. She followed our father to Rabja and there she suffered the worst of her life and lost her first son. She followed our father here in Ageville, and here with her two young children, she faced this danger from an unknown enemy.

She prayed to God for our protection while our two dogs were barking fiercely. Our mother, inside the house, understood that these two devoted dogs would sacrifice their lives to defend us. They would not allow the intruder to enter the compound.

Our mother now thanked our father for bringing two dogs. If he had brought only one dog, the intruder could beat or kill that dog. The bravery of these two dogs prevented the intruder from attacking them. The unknown intruder walked around the fence of the compound, but he couldn't get in. These two dogs fiercely protected their turf.

When the dawn arrived, the dogs stopped barking. Fearing for his life and the consequences of being caught, the potential intruder fled and left. When the dawn morning light started approaching, the neighbors staying in scattered huts came. They came to enquire because they heard the unusual loud barks of the dogs.

Meanwhile, our father also reached home. He could not sleep in his place of work and had a bad dream. While dawn was yet to come, he left and came home. He found our mother and the neighbors discussing the bravery of the dogs.

While having tea which our mother prepared, our father and the neighbors discuss the identity of the unknown would be intruder. Our father told them about the chance encounter on his way and the stranger he met could be the suspect. Since he was unfamiliar with the person, the matter ended there.

Our mother never complained about the incident. There was no resentment that our father left us alone that night. She regarded this incident as an inevitability of living in a remote village. She did her best as a wife and a mother.

This incident changed our mother. She embraced our two dogs as her loyal friends and protectors. They saved our lives, almost sacrificing their own.

In this village, we had varied experiences, with nature, pets and wild animals and human beings. We learned many lessons from these experiences we encountered. But one important thing we learned is that animals would never pretend. They are what they are.

However, human beings are different. There is always something mysterious in their hearts. They have the capabilities to be good and to be bad. They know how to pretend and be hideous.

And then, our father could have decided on the names of the pups. But to make things interesting, he challenged us to make interesting names. He challenged our young minds to think and be creative. This helped us later in life.

While our mother narrated this story to us, our father told us to be wary of strangers. He realized his mistake of telling the unnecessary details to the unknown stranger. There are many things that are better kept within yourself.

He also praised the strength and resilience of our mother. She always has the capability to rise to the occasions. Life is hard and demanding, but our mother did her best to overcome those challenges.

So many times we looked down on many things we underestimate. We never take the time to know and understand their true value. However, frequently, those things we underestimated became our most valuable assets, loyal friends and protectors, like our dogs.

Last but not the least, our father had paid a heavy fine to the bull owner. The bull owner thought to make our family poorer by extortion through tricking and unfair means. However, God answered the prayer of our parents by giving our father this extra job with extra income. God bless our family many folds.

The enemy wanted us to be poorer,

But God would not let that.

We became much richer,

In our body, our mind, and our heart.

6

Lessons from Stolen Fish

TEMPTATIONS ARE EVERYWHERE AND too difficult to conquer.

When I was over six years old, we came back from Ageville and stayed in our mother's village. We came back to enable me to go to a proper day school.

Our parents enrolled me in our mother's village school, one of the best in those days. I studied in this school until I completed my matriculation or standard X.

However, every winter holiday, our father would come home to take me to Ageville, where he taught in the mission morning village school. He took me there to help him on his farm and to teach me many deep and important lessons in life.

There were many stories and life experiences in this small, remote village. I'd like to tell you about another life experience that's truly one-of-a-kind.

My father used to wake up very early in the morning. He would go and work on his small farm very early in the morning. He would take a nap after lunch, as it was difficult to work during daytime because of the humidity and heat.

This morning we woke up early before the sun rose. We prayed our morning prayer together, and had our light breakfast with tea. Then my father left for his field while I had to cook and do other household chores.

Our hut was on top of one small hill, surrounded by beautiful scenery. Downwards from our hut, there is a small river we used to swim, wash our clothes, and fish.

After my father left the house, I cooked, then clean the house and its surrounding areas. When I finished everything, the sun had risen above the hills to the east of the village. I felt hungry, but I had to wait until my father came back from his work.

I was tired of sitting alone in the hut. Therefore, I went to where my father was working in the field. I took the machete along with me. Our father had taught us it was always safe to walk in the jungles of the village with something in your hands to defend yourself. You never knew what animals or snakes you might encounter on the way.

While I was about to cross the river, I saw a small dam upstream that somebody had made. As a young boy, I was curious to know why somebody would make a small dam with twigs, boulders, and leaves. That somebody had made this temporary dam in the shape of a large V.

On careful examination of this temporary dam, I saw a local traditional fish trap, made of bamboo and put it at the lower tip of the V shape dam. The fish-trap was exquisite, made with great craftsmanship.

In addition, the most wonderful thing was that inside the fish trap were about twelve exquisite fish, each about six to seven inches long. These fish were trying to free themselves from the fish trap. They were exquisite to look at.

The sight of those beautiful fish had me captivated instantly. The scene of these fish moving and trying to free themselves from the fish trap was beyond any description. Even as a boy, I knew taking these fish was wrong. But the beauty of these fish and the temptations were beyond me.

I looked around to see if any person was around. There was none I could see except the birds chirping and the sound of the water flowing through the rocks. With my heart pounding, I pried the twigs, small boulders, and leaves with the machete. After I loosened the fish trap, I took away six fish and put them in the bag I carried with me.

Then, I put back the fish-trap along with the remaining fish in the same place exactly, as it was before. I did this so that the owner of the fish trap would not know the difference.

With the fish in my bag, I went to the field where my father was working. With pride, I showed my father the fish I got from the river. I was proud to have so many fish.

"Pa, look, I got so many fish."

"From where did you get them, son?"

"From the river, Pa."

I answered, but from the face of my father, I knew he was unhappy about it.

"Look here, son, those fish are not yours."

My father had seen the temporary dam and the fish trap.

"You should not take those fish. They are not yours."

However, for me, in my boyish adventure, I succumbed to the power of temptations. Since the fish were in the river, I took them. My father, in his wisdom and understanding, admonished me and told me that the person who put the fish trap had worked hard to make the temporary dam and the fish trap.

Then my father continued,

"You should never take what was not yours. If you take a small thing that was not yours, you will graduate to take bigger things. These kinds of things will never end. If you continue, you will only end up in regret."

In my foolishness, I told my father that the fish were small and nobody saw when I took them.

However, my father told me that big or small, and they were not yours. Then, even if no one saw, God sees everything. And the most important thing was that you knew in your heart the fish were not yours.

After my father had admonished me, he left his work and told me to accompany him back to the river. Once there, he told me to put back all the fish inside the fish trap. I looked with envy at the fish, but I had to do what my father told me. From there, we went back to our hut for lunch.

While eating our lunch, we had dried fish with rice. My father looked at me and understood that I missed the fish that we put back in the fish trap. As usual, we took the afternoon siesta and nap.

In the afternoon, my father sensed my disappointment. Therefore, he took the bneij (a local traditional fishing net attached to a pole) and took me to the river. We went downstream from where the temporary fishing trap was.

There he taught me how to catch fishes, which place there were more fishes, and how to use the bneij. There in the river catching fishes, father and son enjoyed the evening together. This was an extremely wonderful day for me.

Before sunset, after we had caught enough fishes, we returned to the hut we call our home. That evening, my father taught me how to clean and roast the bigger fishes so that we can use them in the next few days.

Then, he taught me how to make fish chutney from smaller fishes. We mixed the leftover fresh fishes with onion, ginger, pepper, turmeric, and salt in the banana leaves. Then, we folded the banana leaves and put this inside the traditional clay oven we had burned with firewood earlier. My father knew the exact time when to take out the mixture.

The dinner we had that night was tastier than any food I have ever tasted. However, what was more important to me than the food we ate were the many lessons I learned that day.

First, like those fish, the fish traps of this world, trapped me and many of us. Somebody put the traps in the rivers of life we were swimming. Once caught in the trap, it was difficult to free oneself.

Second, many of those traps are exquisite and beautiful from the outside. Those who make these traps spend much time and labour to make them indistinguishable from the real thing.

Third, many of us succumbed to temptations. It is so easy to be the victim of these temptations. Life would be much better if we could avoid falling to them.

Fourth, never take that which was not yours. If you take them, return them. Because even when nobody sees you, God sees. But most important is that in our hearts, we know we have taken that which was not ours. Never do that which you know is wrong.

Fifth, my father knew how I felt inside. He did not leave me just like that with my disappointment, but he took the time to make me happy, have joy, and be more experienced in life. The bond we had as father and son was very important to me.

Sixth, I have been fortunate to have eaten in some of the best restaurants in and outside the country. However, the food we had that night was the best. The atmosphere of a kerosene lamp-lit dinner in a small hut, clean water and environment, fresh fishes, and the love, joy, and happiness of dining with my father.

Seventh, whatever the circumstances, big or small, life has something to teach us. All of us have our own unique way of living our life. Each of these life's lessons and experiences are unique. It is up to us how we take these lessons.

Eight, the lessons can go on and on, but what I learned that day stood me in good stead in my personal, professional and Christian life.

Throughout these years, I have learned that my father had always done the best for me. His admonitions were for my own good, and his love, care, and understanding in guiding me were beyond words.

If my earthly father had done so much for me, my Heavenly Father is doing much more that words cannot explain. The admonitions were always there, but the joy of fellowship with Him, the peace in my heart, and his blessings in my life surpassed all.

7

The Gun and the Deer

So many times, life threw up things that were difficult to understand. Some of us learnt from these life changing events and some of us don't. Life would have been much better for us if we had taken the time to learn these lessons.

Many of the experiences I had at Ageville were ordinary, but important as lessons of life. Some of these experiences were as if they came from out of this world. This is one of them which I failed to understand its meaning when it happened.

This winter holiday, I went with my father to help him on this farm at Ageville. As the village is so remote, I had the best time of my life there. We lived a life completely in tune with nature.

One morning, my father woke me up early. After our morning prayer and a light breakfast, he left for work on his farm. Before leaving, he gave me the keys to the wooden box where we kept our scant belongings, including the double-barrelled gun. He told me that if I needed to leave the house, I should take the gun along with me.

After he left, I was curious to inspect the gun. I opened the wooden box to make sure that the gun was there. Yes, it was. I knew my father trusted me, but for him to trust me with the gun was too much for me to understand.

After examining the gun, I put it back inside the box. Then, I started cooking, cleaning the house and its adjoining areas. Our small thatched hut lies on top of a hill and I could see for miles around. I could hear the birds chirping in the trees surrounding our house.

When I finished cooking and the household chores, I was in a hurry to leave the house and to carry the gun. I wanted to go to the farm where my father worked. Well, I wanted the villagers to see that I was now a big boy, old enough to carry a real gun. I took the gun from the wooden box and locked it.

I put the gun over my shoulder, closed the door, and left the house. To reach the farm where my father worked, I needed to walk down the hill, cross a small river, and walk along a stretch of jungle.

As I walked down the hill, I was so proud to carry a gun on my shoulder. I felt like a cowboy in a Western film. I wanted the villagers to see me. It would amaze people to see a young boy carrying a real gun.

I crossed the small river, and then the jungle started. Our father had taught us to be alert in the jungle because anything might happen. You never know what you would encounter. There were many wild animals and even snakes.

I was thinking about what I would do if I encountered any wild animal. Could I shoot? What would happen if I missed? Suddenly, I came to a small clearing. There, about twenty or twenty-five feet ahead of me, a deer was grazing.

This was the first time I had seen a deer in the wild. It was beyond words to explain my feelings. Yes, what I wanted had come true. I carried a gun and there in front of me was a deer. It was grazing so near to me, I would not miss shooting it. I took the gun from my shoulder, knelt down, and pointed the gun at the deer.

What did the deer do?

It stopped grazing. Instead of running away, it looked at me. When the deer gazed at me with its deep, piercing eyes, I froze. Its eyes were so beautiful and penetrating that it mesmerized me. For a few moments, the deer gazed intently at me. Then it moved its lips as if it wanted to talk to me. Yes, it talked to me.

What did the deer say to me? You would not believe it, but the deer actually talked to me. Of course, not in human language but in a kind of sacred communication that both of us could understand.

"Dear boy, I know you have a gun. I know guns are dangerous. However, you are just a small young boy carrying a gun. Shoot me if you dare."

I looked at the gun. Yes, I had a gun, a double-barrelled one. Yes, in front of me was a wild deer. It was the greatest opportunity I would receive in my lifetime. I would tell my father and all the villagers that I shot and killed the deer with my father's gun. I was too excited to know what to do when the deer started talking again.

"Look, dear boy, I know what you feel. You may think that I am just a wild animal, but I know when there is danger. All animals know when there is danger in their life. I saw you walking with the gun, but I know you cannot harm me. You don't have the power to kill me."

"How do you know?"

"In human language you have a word, 'instinct.' That is what you call it, 'instinct.' We animals also have 'instinct.' We know who can harm us and who cannot."

"Tell me more."

"Oh yes, your father is a wise man. I wish there were more fathers like him. Your father has taught you many important lessons of life, including giving you a real gun to carry.

Most fathers do not understand that they are giving their children dangerous things, to play with, real or psychological guns. With such guns, they kill not only animals but their fellow human beings as well. And finally, they may kill themselves."

"Yes, I am listening."

"Human beings kill us innocent animals. We do not harm human beings, but they kill us. Other wild animals will not kill us unless they are hungry. They do not kill us for fun. Only human beings kill us for fun.

Humans have so many good and tasty foods on their plates, but they treat our meat, as a delicacy. You know, they are not only killing us, but if they continue to degrade and spoil the environment with their greed, they will eventually kill themselves."

"Oh yes, we learn that at school."

"Dear boy, what you learn has no impact. Practice what you learn, and only then will the world be a better place. Learn to protect us wild animals, so that you protect yourselves.

Please send the message to the entire world that they should not kill us. Let us co-exist, wild animals and human beings. That is one of the ways to save mother earth. Please send this message. It is very important."

"I am too small to tell the world. And the world may not listen to me."

"If they do not listen, that is up to them. Your responsibility is to tell the world about the dangers of environmental degradation. Future generations will blame you for the destruction of mother Earth."

"Okay, I will do my best. I will tell the world."

"Before we parted, please promise not to kill any wild animal or bird."

Many times my parents made me promise not to do those silly and serious mistakes we made as children. If I made those promises to my parents, then why not to the deer?

Therefore, without thinking far and the consequences, I said,

"Yes, I promise."

"Good. Then it is time for me to leave. Bye."

At this, the deer jumped from where it was grazing and vanished into the thick jungle.

Was I in a dream? Was it really that the deer talked to me?

I pinched myself. Yes, I was not dreaming, but I had really met and talked with the wild deer. Yes, it did not talk to me in human language but a kind of sacred communication, which only the deer and I could understand.

With a sense of wonder and awe, I continued my journey to where my father worked. I kept thinking of what the deer had communicated to me.

Could we make the world a better place? Could humans and wild animals co-exist? While preoccupied with my thoughts, I reached the field where my father worked.

Excitedly, I told him about the deer and the way it communicated to me. He understood. Yes, he agreed wild animals could communicate with humans, but only under special circumstances and purpose. God can use many ways to communicate with us human beings.

I asked him why the deer had shown no fear. Why had it not run away from me?

Then my father said,

"I have been planning to give you some deep and important lessons in life. This morning I took a chance. I told you to bring the gun along with you. At your age, a gun with bullets is too dangerous. Therefore, I removed the bullets. The deer knew that the gun you carried had no bullet."

"What and how?"

With a smiling face, he opened his old bag and showed me. There, inside the old rusty bag, were the shiny bullets.

Countless times, my friends from the village jeered and were angry at me.

Why did my friends get angry and jeered at me?

As young village boys, we would go together to hunt small wild animals and birds. When I saw the animal or bird in danger, I would trample a twig or make a discreet sound to make the animal or bird aware of our presence, making them flee or fly away from the dangers.

I have never done this intentionally or on purpose, it just came naturally to me. Sometimes, I wondered and asked myself why I always did like this? Perhaps the promise I made to the deer not to kill animals or birds was always there, somewhere deep in my subconscious mind.

Many times I questioned why God had not given me the power to do those things I wanted to do. I wanted to do many things to satisfy my ego and to impress the world.

But God had taken away those deadly bullets from me because He wanted me, not to be an instrument to hurt or kill, but an instrument to love and care.

8

How I Carry the Tortoise

I FOUND AN EXOTIC thing in an exotic place. An ecstatic feeling in winning the battle of wits.

Many of the experiences I had and the lessons I learned in Ageville in those years were beyond description. This is yet another wonderful and meaningful story.

Both my father and I woke up early before the sun rose. Then we sat down for our morning prayer. We had our light breakfast and morning tea and after that, my father left for his work on his field on the other side of the river.

In the deep forest, a little farther from our hut, I heard the apes (hoolock gibbon) singing. Every morning, it is their ritual to sing, telling the world that they have woken up.

After I finished the household chores, the sun had risen above the hills. So, I left for the field where my father worked. As taught by him, I carried the machete to protect myself in case of any eventualities. I bolted the hut and left.

I sauntered down the hill, enjoying the morning breeze and the scenery. While enjoying my walk, I reached the bank of the river. When I was crossing the river, I saw the tortoise on the golden sandy beach a few feet from me.

The tortoise crawled across the sand to get to the water. The colour of the tortoise was golden brown, matching the colour of the golden sand. This tortoise was of medium size.

I felt thrilled to discover this tortoise in its natural habitat. I raced to the place where the tortoise was crawling. With the machete, I tapped its shell. When I tapped it, the tortoise retracted and buried its head and feet under the shell. It stopped crawling.

Nobody told me, but I perceived that if the tortoise reached the water, it could swim in the deep water. If the tortoise swam, catching it would be impossible for me. The tortoise knew this. Therefore, the tortoise tried its best to reach the safety of the river.

I stood behind the tortoise to prevent it from biting me. After some time, the tortoise opened its head and started crawling towards the water.

When I saw this, I again tapped the tortoise with the machete. After a light tap, the tortoise pulled back its head and legs under the shell. Then I pushed it with the machete a little farther away from the river.

Here in the sand, near the river, we played our little game of life and death. The tortoise, as if knowing the danger it faced, tried with all its ability to reach the water.

After opening its head, it attempted to crawl towards the water. But when it opened its head, I tapped it with the machete. When the tortoise withdrew its head and legs inside its shell, I pushed it back further from the river.

I used all my abilities to catch and carry this tortoise home. My plan was to lift the tortoise, but not using my bare hands. I knew the risks of touching it. It could bite me, and its bite was dangerous.

I recalled the story my father once told me. One day in the market, some soldiers came to the place where they sold tortoises. With curiosity, a soldier played and kick a tortoise with his boot.

The tortoise he played with bit his boot. The soldier screamed in agony as the tortoise sunk its teeth into his boot and toe. From the bitten boot, blood was dripping. The soldier could free himself from the tortoise's bite after a tough struggle.

Thus, I was aware of the dangers of touching the tortoise with my bare hands. Despite the dangers, I did not want to let this tortoise go free. I wanted to carry and take it home as a trophy.

The big question now was how to carry this tortoise to our hut?

We played this game of "cat and mouse" for a long time. The tortoise tried to reach the river to free itself from me while I tried to push it away from the river to the sand. The sand impeded the tortoise's movement. Therefore, I had the advantage.

Then I recalled the words of wisdom our father once told us. Do not concentrate on the problem. Always try to think and find the solution. If I continue to focus on the problem, it will remain a problem forever.

I had to think about the solution. I tried to find a solution using this novel approach. The machete was in my hand. This would aid me in finding a solution.

With this new insight, I tried putting the machete below the belly of the tortoise and lifted it. However, I could not balance the machete with the tortoise. When the tortoise moved, it fell to the ground.

If it was just land, I could use the machete to push the tortoise uphill to our hut. But there is a river to cross. How do you get the tortoise across the river?

Once the tortoise reached the water, it would swim and vanish. All my hard work would be for nothing. So, there had to be other options.

Next to the beach I fought with the tortoise, was a jungle where trees of all sizes grew. After looking at these trees, I found my-eureka moment.

After much thought, I've come up with the solution. I tapped the tortoise's shell, causing it to pull its head and legs inside. Then I used the machete to push the tortoise as far inland as I could. I dashed into the jungle in search of a tree that matched.

Not just any tree, but the one with two branches that can support the tortoise. While in search of the right tree, I kept my eyes on the tortoise as well. The tortoise could crawl and reach the river. If it reached the water, my plans would be in vain.

Meanwhile, I had identified the most suitable tree. The tree had a trunk and two equal size branches big enough to hold the tortoise.

Once I had pushed the tortoise away from the river, I sprinted to the jungle to cut down this tree. Now I had the most suitable tree for my plan. I came back to where the tortoise was and tapped its shell.

By using the machete, I placed the cut tree beside the tortoise. With my left hand, I grasp the tree trunk from below. With my right hand using the machete, I pulled the tortoise to become entwined in the trunk with its two branches.

I carried the tortoise, using my left hand to hold the tree trunk and my right hand, to use the machete as a wrench to secure it. It worked, hooray, my plan worked!

To carry the tortoise this way was difficult. The weight of the tortoise strained my muscles. The tortoise attempted to free itself by moving. It couldn't bite me in that position, though. I carried the tortoise this way, but I had to trudge.

The toughest part was the river. How can I cross the river holding the tortoise this way? If the tortoise fell in the water while I was crossing, my efforts would be in vain.

With every ounce of energy and intense concentration, I crossed the river while holding the tortoise in a tree trunk with two branches. Somehow, I reached the other side of the bank. Despite being tired, my plan had succeeded.

Carrying the tortoise up the winding path to our hut was difficult and exhausting. I had to rest and set down the tortoise every ten or fifteen steps. The walk back home was tedious and slow.

When I was two-thirds of the way home, I took a rest. The sun had risen and was shining directly overhead. The heat of the sun made me sweat profusely. I felt tired and hungry.

When I looked at the golden brown wild tortoise, I thought of setting it free. So many troubles just to carry a tortoise home.

While I was taking a rest on the path, I saw my father coming back from work in the field to have lunch. I was proud of my ability to catch the tortoise and carry it in my own unique way. As he neared, I shouted,

"Pa, look! I got a tortoise from the sand near the river."

With surprise, my father observed the tortoise entangled in the tree with two branches. As he was about to ask me what happened, I explained how I carried the tortoise.

He smiled at my boyish ingenuity and said,

"Son, there is a better way to carry the tortoise."

"How? Please show me."

He took the machete from me and used it to flip the tortoise upside down. After flipping the tortoise over, he gently placed his hands beneath its shell.

While showing me this, he said,

"Son, once you flip the tortoise over, it will stay that way forever. You can carry or do whatever you want to the tortoise, but it can never bite you from that position.

It is a problem for you, but to me, it is simple. There's always a better way, if you know how. Listen and learn from the wisdom of elders."

"Thank you, Pa."

With my father's guidance, I slowly placed both hands below the tortoise's shell. Under my palms, I felt the weight, patches, and patterns of the shell of this golden brown tortoise. It is difficult to describe my excitement in carrying the tortoise this way.

No more dangers, no more difficulties, but safe and easy. The rest of the journey back home was enjoyable as I held the flipped-over tortoise in my hands.

I spent countless hours trying to figure out how to carry the tortoise. I carried it with great difficulty and fear. However, my father did it in seconds, so simple, with confidence and without fear.

I had invested an immeasurable amount of time trying to determine the most optimum way to live my life. I attempted multiple methods but found it too challenging to continue. But when I surrender my life to God, my Heavenly Father, I discover that the journey of life is breath-taking and invigorating.

9

Lessons from Carrying the Tortoise

SLAVERY IS PREVALENT IN *many forms, visible and invisible. However, freedom is intrinsic to human beings, and also to animals.*

To this day, I still remember how I felt the texture of the shell of the golden brown tortoise I hold in my hands. The walk from that spot my father showed me how to carry the tortoise up to our hut was full of joy and excitement. Those were the experiences that you treasure for a lifetime.

I did not realize how situations changed. A few minutes ago, with my own efforts, I struggled with all my power to hold and carry the tortoise. It was an arduous journey up the winding and uphill path, each step slow and laborious. The trek was too tiresome and I almost quit.

But now, after I learned from my father the right way to carry the tortoise, it was simple and easy. The walk back home was exhilarating and joyful. No more sweats, no more hardships, but overjoyed. It was one of the most memorable walks I had ever taken.

When we reached home, I asked my father where to keep the tortoise. He told me to put the tortoise upside down anywhere and it could never escape. I put the tortoise in the upside-down position in the corner of our hut and covered it with an empty bamboo basket upside down.

That night, I thought about my experiences of getting the tortoise from the beach near the river and carried it home. Yes, my improvised style of carrying it was difficult, but at least I did it.

I realized I was a young boy not as well experienced in the matter of learning life's lessons as my father. It was fun, wonderful and an adventure to have lived this kind of life with my father. With these thoughts, I fall asleep.

The next morning, I opened the bamboo basket to see the tortoise. It was still lying in the upside-down position. After looking at the tortoise, I saw it completely dried up.

What affected me more was the head and neck. It hanged up there with nothing to support. I knew it could breathe, but that was all it did. That was the life of this poor little tortoise.

That day, I accompanied my father to help him on his field. But my mind was with the tortoise. Maybe it was thirsty, maybe it was hungry?

We eat our food at least three times a day. We fed our livestock, goats, dogs, hens, and cocks every day. How can we leave the tortoise like that without feeding it?

That evening, coming back from the farm, when we reached home, I opened the bamboo basket and looked at the tortoise. It was there, but it looked pitiful and barely alive. It did not make any movement except its eyes were half-opened.

Despite being exhausted from the day's work, I found it difficult to sleep that night. I was thinking about this tortoise. Deep in my heart, I knew it was an enormous achievement for me.

I thought I would tell my friends and peers about this brilliant experience of carrying a tortoise. Not only would I tell them, but I could also show them the golden-brown shell of the tortoise as evidence.

The next morning, after I woke up, I again opened the bamboo basket to look at the tortoise. Yes, it was still there in the same position we kept it. But looking at its legs, neck, and head sticking upside down, tears fell from my eyes.

What if I was in that position and nobody would help me? I was in two minds. An exotic trophy to show off and also a sense of pity for the helpless tortoise.

On the third night, I told my father about my dilemma. He told me we could do two things.

One, kill it, eat its meat as a delicacy, and keep the shell as a trophy.

Second, release it back to the wild. You would lose the tortoise, but you would get peace of mind. It would be an unforgettable experience for you.

I found it difficult to decide, but then I remembered my promise to the deer: I will not kill another wild animal or bird. There and then, I made my decision. With great reluctance and a sense of loss, I said to my father,

"Pa, let's release the tortoise back to the river."

The next morning and with deep pain in my heart, I put my hands under the shell of the tortoise and carried it. Accompanied by my father, we walked down the slope from our hut to the river.

When we reached the river, I put the shell of the tortoise in the water. Then, with a painful heart, I turned the tortoise upside down, back to its original position, and released it into the water.

The tortoise swam with all its four legs and its head. While it swam, it looked as if it was telling me,

"I am alive. I am free. I am alive, I am free."

Then it swam gracefully and disappeared into the deep water of the river.

Now that I am a grownup, I learned many lessons from this unique experience. These are some of them:

Many things in life seemed complex. But to the experts, those things were simple. When faced with problems, I have learned to seek help and advice from elders, experts, and even from my juniors who knew the subject well. To progress in life, I need the help of others.

Second, I have been walking along this journey, on the beautiful path called life. On crossing the river, at a certain point in life, and on its bank and sand, I found golden, beautiful, exotic things.

I found trophies, achievements, fame, honour, pride, pleasures, positions, money, and more. It was exhilarating to carry them with my efforts and capabilities. I was proud to carry and show them off.

Then one day, I realized these loads were too heavy for me to carry. I suffered from stress, depression, and many ailments because the loads I carried were too heavy. The path I travelled was difficult.

Then, when I was too tired and was about to quit, I heard that small silent voice whispered in my heart,

"Son, you are carrying these loads the wrong way. There is a better way. Flip over those loads upside down. Put them in the right perspective."

I resisted. I was too proud to let go. But later on, I realized I could never proceed ahead in life with these loads in my life. I had to choose. At last, I turned them upside down. This journey I call life is now light and very exciting.

The other lesson was to let go. There are many things and possessions we wanted to keep as trophies to show off. However, if those things disturb your conscience, it is better to let go.

I found it so hard to let go of the tortoise. I also found it so hard to let go of many things in my life. But somehow I did let go of many of those things. My action saved the poor tortoise and brought me rich experiences in this journey of life. It brought me joy and peace.

There are other lessons, but one of the most important was that my life had been like this tortoise.

I had just got out of the woods of life. I saw the beautiful river at the edge of the beach and I wanted to swim there. Therefore, I crawled slowly on the sandy beach enjoying the bright sunshine.

Then I saw the shadow and had a gentle tap on my back. I did not realize it was the enemy. I fought for my life, but the stronger force overpowered me.

Things of this world carried and kept me upside down in the dark cover of the bamboo basket. I was thirsty, but there was no water for my heart and soul. I was hungry, but no food could satisfy me. The darkness of the bamboo basket world enveloped me.

I tried to crawl, but I realized I was upside down. I was supposed to stand erect and walk on my feet, but I was lying upside down. There was no way to free myself.

All I could do was cry out for help, not only with the words of my mouth, but with the deep, silent sound of my heart. After I cried out, I realized there were gentle Hands that carried me to the place I belonged.

Then I realized the unseen powerful hands of God carried me. This Higher Power took me from utter helplessness and darkness to bright sunlight. He gently carried me along the way to that crystal clear beautiful river, where He released me from bondage to freedom.

Now I can swim in this river of life and shout with joy,

"I am alive. I am free! Now I am alive and I am free."

There are many descriptions of hell, but nothing compared to my experience. Inside that darkness covered by a bamboo basket, a flip over or upside down life was a true torment in hell.

There are many descriptions of Heaven, and I experienced those joys of being there. Swimming gleefully and freely in the river of life is heaven to me.

Now that I have experienced both heaven and hell, I thank God for allowing me to go through those experiences, and for saving me from hell's torment, and leading me to the happiness of Heaven.

10

The Paddy Field

CREATIVITY IS A PART of the human psyche. Could I help and have a hand in creating something nice, good, and productive?

Many paddy or rice fields, big and small, dotted the landscape here in Ageville. When I look at them, I can't take my eyes off those beautiful fields, especially before the harvest.

These rice fields were so captivating to look at. It reminded me that there must be someone who saw the barren land and converted that into those beautiful paddy fields.

I had witnessed the challenging process of transforming a muddy swamp into a picturesque paddy field. I had contributed to creating a paddy field, no matter how small my help was. From the making of this beautiful paddy field, I learned many valuable life lessons.

There was a marshy swamp located a little far from our father's farm. A flowing stream ran through the middle of the swamp. This land was the property of the Raid or a community land.

One day, while burning to make charcoal in the nearby forest, our father asked me to accompany him to survey this marshy swamp. This was the first time I went to survey the area up close. The entire area was a swampy mud-land filled with small trees, shrubs, and diverse tropical plants and weeds.

That night, at our little hut we called home, our father was deep in thought. Then, before we went to sleep, he said,

"Son, I think we can convert that marshy swamp into a paddy field."

When our father looked at me, I said,

"But it is a muddy swamp full of trees, tropical plants and weeds."

"I know, but with hard work and perseverance, we can transform that swamp into a fertile paddy field. If we can convert the swamp into a paddy field, we can sow paddy. Given the field's size, I believe we can cultivate and get enough rice to feed our whole family."

I was then too young to understand. I couldn't grasp the significance of this project in my mind. To me, it would be a daunting task, if not impossible. It would take years to get the desired results.

However, to our father's sharp mind, this would bring positive changes to many things. It will change his family's economic conditions, the landscape, the village, and his world as a teacher.

As the land is community land, our father requested the village durbar to give this muddy swamp to him. Some members laughed at our father for asking for such a useless marshy swamp.

People avoided such swamps as they believed that from such swamps, malaria emanated and spread.[1] The villagers, in those days, believed that an evil entity called Rih lived in such swamps. If you disturb this Rih, malaria would follow.

However, other village elders believed that if they could convert all these swamps into productive fields, the evil entity Rih, the originator of malaria, would have no place to live. If it had no place to live, then it would die a natural death.

Or if this Rih had no place to live, it would have to flee and live somewhere else. This would make the village malaria free, more beautiful, and more productive. It will make the village a healthier place to live.

Most of these village elders wanted to get rid of these dangerous and unproductive swamps and make them all productive. Therefore, the village durbar gladly gave this swamp and its adjoining areas to our father.

In the first year, our father built a dam from the upper source of the stream. He did not have money to buy cement. Even if he had the money, the cost would be exorbitant, as it had to be carried by people over a long distance. So, he used only the materials available there.

---

1. It's proved by science that swamps are breeding grounds for mosquitoes which these villagers knew long ago.

He constructed the dam using bare traditional implements, like a spade and crowbar. Then he dug a small ditch-like channel from the western side of the swamp. He made the ditch around the swamp so that he can divert the water from the stream to flow from the side of the swamp instead of from the middle.

In the first year, I helped him in whatever capacity I could. I helped in digging the ditch, collecting small boulders and stones to make a dam from the starting point of the swamp. It was excruciating hard work.

After building a small dam, he diverted the water to the drain he made. During the winter months, it was fine. However, the dam he constructed was not strong enough for the current and the rain water during the monsoon. It was during the summer that heavy rainfall with a strong current overran this small dam and destroyed everything.

After this unfortunate incident, I thought our father would stop his endeavor, but this made him more determined to overcome the challenges. From what happened, he told me he had a better idea of how to construct a dam.

He rebuilt the dam. It was here that I saw my father's ingenuity and amateur engineering skills. With materials like boulders, stones, logs, soil, sticks, branches of trees, he made this dam.

Apart from his school duties, he spent his time converting this swamp into a cultivable paddy field. It amazed me that this second dam withstood the ravage of the flood water during the summer months.

During heavy rains, others would rest because they could not work, but our father would take this opportunity to make the drain bigger and reclaim the swamp. By using his spade and crowbar, he would use the water current to chop the soil. The water current would carry this soil downstream, making the drain bigger, thus enlarging the cultivable area of the swamp.

Every winter, after the holidays from school, I would accompany him to help him with this endeavor. I enjoyed working with him. I would help him in cutting the trees, the shrubs, removing the tropical plants and weeds.

After we had cleared part of the swamp, we carried the soil from the adjacent area and filled the swamp with topsoil. It was very hard work.

In the next year, we could only clean the area and rebuild the dam which the strong current destroyed. So there was no paddy field to show. However, in the third year, we could build a few small patches for the sowing of rice. Our father was ecstatic with this small progress.

Every year, we kept on adding some patches to the existing field. From his meagre salary and income, our father could not employ any helper or laborer. So, he did everything by himself. I could help him only during those winter months of the school holidays.

Each year we could add a new channel where we could plant paddy seeds. After over seven long years of hard work, the swamp became a developed paddy field. It was so beautiful to look at.

Our father was so proud that through his bare hands and with the most basic of tools, he could convert the marshy swamp into a beautiful paddy field.

Despite looking good to the eyes, our father knew it needed proper maintenance. So, now and then, he would look for any sign of crack or damage in the dam or the plots. If he found any small crack or damage, he would repair and make this field a beautiful paddy field.

Whenever we came home from Ageville, we carried rice in sacks to the nearest village about one hour's walk away. From there, we would catch any vehicles coming to the city and then to our home. It was a long way, but we were happy because that rice meant staple food for the family.

Now, looking at those exquisite paddy fields reminded me of those years where our father taught me many important things in life. It taught me hard work, the dignity of labor, and perseverance.

There would be failures, setbacks, disappointments, but never lose hope. Continue your hard work, because one day, no matter how long, success will come.

Now, I look at many beautiful things: a paddy field, an orchard, a school building, a college, a university, and many other beautiful things from a different perspective. These remind me that someone saw the possibilities and dared to dream that beautiful things were possible.

Those who saw the possibilities did not leave just like that, but they took action and worked hard. They work hard to realize those dreams to make the future and this world a better place.

Our father worked so hard. He suffered from chronic malaria but left a legacy for us and our children because he saw that through his hard work, our future would be brighter.

On reflection, I discovered that my life resembles this paddy field. Sometimes, only insignificant things like tiny trees, shrubs, and useless plants and weeds grew. Then mosquitoes and other evil entities made this life a breeding ground.

However, I tried to make my life a beautiful and productive field. At first, it was difficult to get rid of the useless shrubs and weeds and to stop the breeding of mosquitoes and evil entities inside my heart. But my Heavenly Father helped me in my endeavor.

There were failures, setbacks, obstacles and many problems to make this life productive and beautiful. Sometimes the flood overran the dams and boundaries I constructed.

However, from these failures and mistakes, I learned to make better and stronger dams and boundaries to guard myself. To make my life productive and beautiful, I must also look for any minor damages or small cracks in my character and repair them immediately.

To get a bountiful harvest in life, first, I must convert my mind-set from a swamp to a field, then I must plough and prepare that field, fertilize the soil, sow the good seeds, nurture the seedlings and plants, take out the weeds, guard against any destruction by the forces of the enemies.

It is hard work, but I can tell you; it's worth all those troubles because this is the best life I can live. Humanly, it may not be possible for me to live this kind of life but with God, everything is possible.

11

Fighting the Big Black Bear with Words

I KNOW WORDS HAVE power, but to witness the magical power of words was beyond words.

My father and I were busy transforming the swamp into a paddy field. There were many things that needed to be done. Because we concentrated so much on our work, we forgot the time.

We had many things left to do, but we noticed the sun had almost set on the horizon. All the farmers had ceased their works and left their fields. They respect the sun and work mostly in daylight.

Village folks out here think that only bad people, thieves and robbers, work in the darkness or night time. Out here, the people believe God created the day to work and the night to rest. They believed this and did their best.

When we realized that the sun had almost set, we hurried ourselves to put all the things in the proper place. We put the fire-woods we had cut inside the ratab (a traditional wood and bamboo tool with a head strap used for carrying many things, including fire-woods).

As we were in a hurry, our father put the machete inside the ratab. He then carried this ratab full of fire-woods in his back. He used the walking stick to aid him in walking the winding path.

I carried an old bag holding the bottle-gourd where we kept our drinking water, father's smoking pipe, a small knife and other small stuff. I also hold the walking stick in my right hand.

It was dusk, where the sun had almost set, but total darkness was yet to set in. It was the most pleasant time to return home, even where the place we call home was a small but beautiful hut. This was also the most dangerous time to walk. Wild animals came out from their hiding places, roaming the jungles, searching for food.

We had almost reached the small river where I fought and released the tortoise when my father signalled for me to stop. He overtook me and told me to walk closely behind him while he walked in front of me. I thought of asking why, but I just obeyed him because our father would do nothing without a valid reason.

We crossed the river and were walking up the winding path. My father was in front of me while I followed him from behind. With no warning, about thirty feet ahead of us, the big black bear appeared. It was about to cross the path we were walking.

When this big black bear saw us, it howled and stood on its hind legs. With its sharp nails and front legs, it opened up to attack us. While howling, it came towards us. Its black hairs standing from head to toe. At this sight, my whole body shook. My hairs stood from tremendous fear.

I knew the big black bear would attack us. At this moment, my father used his left arm to stop me from proceeding. With his right hand holding the walking stick, he lifted it and swung in such a way to hit the big black bear. But this was not all. What he did at this moment was unexpected and beyond description.

While lifting the walking stick, he shouted at the top of his voice, "*Common now Big Black Bear. Come and fight with me if you dare. Are you courageous enough to fight like a man? Common, common, come let us fight. If you can fight with me, come forward. If you dare not fight, run away to the jungle.*

I am a man. You are an animal. An animal cannot win against me, a human being. Come near, I will beat you black and blue. Attack me and I will kill you. Run away and you are safe. This is human territory. Your territory is in the jungle. So, if you do not want to get hurt, get out of the way. Run away or I will kill you!"

I could not believe my eyes and my ears. It was too eerie and out of this world. When my father shouted, the big black bear froze. It stopped in its tracks. It appeared confused. The big black bear put down its front legs to the ground.

The bear, as a hurt battered, lost boxer, lowering its head, it walked away from us to the jungle. While we stood our ground, the big black bear disappeared into the jungle.

When there was no more danger and all was clear, we proceeded to our house. We walked slowly, climbing the wingding path to our hut. I was still shivering from the shock of encountering the big black bear which almost attacked us. Silence enveloped the walk back home.

We cooked our food and had our dinner. We sat by the fire silently while the kerosene lamp shone inside our small hut. After our prayer, we went to sleep. But I could not sleep despite being tired from the hard-day's work. I kept thinking about the encounter with the big black bear.

What I was thinking, I could no longer keep it within myself. While I was lying in the bed, I asked my father,

"Pa, did you know in advance that the bear would come when you sent me to walk behind you?"

"Last night I had an unpleasant dream," he said, "and while we were walking in the dusk, I had a hunch that something bad was going to happen. I did not want you to get hurt. I walked ahead of you to protect you."

"What about you shouting at the top of your voice at the big black bear?"

What he told me that night was beyond description and would remain with me forever. These are the words he told me and said,

"Son, words are the most powerful tool God gave human beings. It is the greatest arsenal we have in our possession. We have many differences with animals but the greatest difference is words and the ability to speak.

Our life is according to the words we speak. I am not, I cannot, I will not—if you use and keep on speaking these words, you will be like that. I am, I can or I will, make all the difference. If you speak only about failures, you cannot expect to win. If you speak negative things, you cannot expect positive things.

Words are like seeds. Farmers plant only good seeds. You plant pleasant words; you reap a good life. If you planted bad words, you reaped a terrible life. The fruits of life are what you planted, whether good or bad.

Son, remember that we bless with words and curse also with words. Many people do not understand that they curse themselves and their life with their words. I will not get that job, I will not get that house or I will not be healthy. These are the words we curse ourselves. Whichever words you speak, it will surely come true.

Words can be your friends or your enemies. It is not the enemies that stop you from progress, but your own words. Many times, we blame others for what happens to us, but in reality, we should blame ourselves for the way we use words. In times of need, if we know how to use words, they are our defense and best friends.

Words can change you and can change others for good or for bad. Words can lead you to the top and words can throw you to the bottom. With words, we can change others as well as ourselves. With words, we can break or heal our hearts. Words are our strength and words are also our weaknesses.

We can define a person with words. You can identify me as your father with words. You can call me father, with words. I can explain myself with words. If I can control the words I speak, I can control anything in my life. Words are free, but it costs us everything.

Therefore, son, please use your words wisely. When you grow up, be responsible for the words you speak. Use proper words. Speak the truth. Control your tongue. Speak with humility. Remember, your success, power, respect, dignity, honour depend on the words you speak."

"But how did you know that the big black bear would obey you by shouting with words?"

"I told you we can tame the fiercest animals with words. All animals have an instinct and are afraid of human beings. The main reason they are afraid is because we could speak while they could not. My father taught me all these things. I also learned the power of words from the Bible.

And since the best tool to fight is words—that is what I did. I didn't plan it that way. It just came with my instinct. The best thing was that, as you have seen, it worked. The big black bear was confused when it saw and heard me shouting at it.

If I fought with the walking stick, the bear would have fought back with me. It was life and death for both sides. Usually, bears would never quit when they fought. They would rather die fighting.

By shouting at the bear, we both win. The big black bear fled to its natural habitat. For you and me, we could walk back home safely. That is the best way to fight when both are winners.

The bear did not plan to attack us; it was searching for food walking this way. We did not plan to hunt and kill the bear. It was an accident that the bear crossed our path.

Therefore, when you fight with wisdom, both the fighting parties are winners. When you use your words wisely, all will be winners.

On the importance of words, King David said, "Set a guard, O Lord, over my mouth; keep watch over the door of my lips!"[1]

On the beauty of words, King Solomon said, "A word fitly spoken is like apples of gold in settings of silver. Like an earring of gold and an ornament of fine gold is a wise rebuker to an obedient ear."[2]

And on the power of words, James said, "If anyone does not stumble in words, he is a perfect man, able also to bridle the whole body. . . . . And the tongue is a fire, a world of iniquity. The tongue is so set among our members that it defiles the whole body, and sets on fire the course of nature; and it is set on fire by hell."[3]

1. Ps.141:3
2. Prov.25:11–12
3. Jas.3:2—6

12

A Fistful of Rice

IF YOU GIVE, YOU shall receive. But how much is too small to give to God?

The fire was burning in the hearth, and the kerosene lamp shone, making beautiful shadows of everything. The fire in the hearth, the lamp in its stand, and the words from my father's mouth were as if synchronized to make things beautiful.

In a relaxed atmosphere, father and son discussed together the important and deeper things of life. Life is not only to work, to get the food we eat and to live. Life is also about those beautiful things which build our bodies, enrich our minds, and satisfy our souls.

After working so hard the entire day, I looked forward to the storytelling session with my father. After finishing our dinner and before we took complete rest for our tired bodies, we enjoyed the time for those beautiful ideas and concepts that enrich the souls.

"Last night I told you how I lost my first wife to death and my sons to traditions. That changed everything in my life and made me become a schoolteacher. You want to know how I started my vocation as a schoolteacher, don't you?"

My father asked me, but without waiting for my answer, he said, "I want to start from the very beginning.

This evening, before you cook rice, what did you do before putting the rice in the cooking pot?" he asked me.

Before I put the rice into the cooking pot, what did I do? Then I remembered the ritual. I told him,

"I took a fistful of rice and put it separately in another container,"

"Why are you doing it?"

"I don't know, Pa,"

I had seen my parents do this every day. Every time before they cook rice, they put a fistful of rice in a special container. When I was old enough to learn to cook, they told me to do the same. So, in our house, whenever we cook rice, before we wash and put the rice in the cooking pot, we put aside a fistful of rice in a special container.

This had become a ritual. Every week, on Sunday morning, somebody from the church would come to collect this rice we set aside. I never questioned this ritual. It never occurred to me to ask about it. There are things in life which you just follow or do, asking no questions.

"Son, for everything that you do, you should know why you are doing it. Every time we cook rice, we put aside a fistful of rice in the special container. There is a powerful reason for this ritual. Let me tell you how all this started."

Then he told me this wonderful story.

There was one person, Mr. Gatphoh, who heard about this idea that there were people who set aside a fistful of rice every time they cooked their rice. They gave this rice they set aside for the use of the church. This idea of a fistful of rice to set aside stuck with him.

This man was a prominent government official looking after schools. He saw first-hand the conditions of the schools in those days. There were very few schools, especially in remote and far-flung areas. People needed education, but there was a shortage of funds to establish and run these schools.

He wanted to spread education by setting up schools in remote and far-flung villages. After praying and pondering on this issue, he took up the idea of raising funds through this fistful of rice with the church to which he belonged. At first, there were objections and resistance. Some people argued that giving a fistful of rice to God was too little to give.

However, he persevered with this idea. He started experimenting with this in his own house. Every day his wife would keep separately a fistful of rice when they cooked rice. At the end of the week, he measured the rice set aside and found that it was more than half a kilogram.

Then, he requested his near relatives to do the same. After that, he told his friends and known associates. Then, finally, he convinced the church about the importance and benefit of this endeavor. He clarified that if one family could contribute a minimum of half a kg of rice per week, then if you take twenty families, the rice collected per week would be ten kilograms. Then for one month, it would be forty kilograms. Sell this rice and the funds from there could establish and run schools.

As with any new and innovative idea, it was slow to catch on. However, once the people accepted this, the idea gained widespread popularity thereafter. Thanks to this innovative idea, the church raised a sizable amount of funds. From these funds, they established schools.

The church's highest authority, at last, took up this issue. After deliberations, they accepted this innovative idea to raise funds, especially for establishing and running of schools. They instructed all the churches under their control to implement this innovative idea. People happily accepted this noble idea.

So, my father's church, combined with a few other churches, which they called a sub-district, implemented this idea to raise funds. They raised enough funds by collecting and selling this fistful of rice to support those existing schools and also to start new schools.

In those days, there were many villages where there was no school. But finally, the church authority selected one remote village about half an hour's walk from my father's village. When all things were in place, they appointed my father to be the pioneer teacher in this morning's school.

He continued with this story, saying, "So, dear son, when you set aside that fistful of rice to give to God through the church, please remember the importance and significance of this humble act. There are many lessons to learn, but let me enumerate these few.

First, it is an act of love. God is the source of everything. All the blessings that we get and have are from God. If you love someone, you would do good things for that someone. If you love God, do something good for God daily.

Second, it is an act of gratitude. We get this life and everything from God. You cannot repay all that you get from God. But this act of giving a fistful of rice reminds us of our gratefulness to God.

Third, it is an act of relationship. How do you relate to God? You relate with God by doing things that please God. We are poor; we do not have great things to do for God, but the least we can do is give a fistful of rice whenever we cook rice.

Fourth, a good habit. You form a habit by doing it daily. You make a good habit by giving something to God daily, even when what you give is tiny.

Fifth, it does not affect the quantity of rice we eat, but it affects the quality of life we live. A fistful of rice does not make any difference to the overall quantity, but it makes you happy because you are doing something for God.

Sixth, it is easy to do. People avoided doing the thing because it was hard. But giving a fistful of rice is easy. All rich and poor, educated and uneducated, big or small families can do this act of giving. There is no discrimination, all are equal and give equally.

Seventh, an act of obedience. How do you show your obedience to God, our Creator? You show your obedience by doing those small things every day.

Eight, an act of responsibility. Giving a fistful of rice is an act of collective responsibility towards the church and the overall development of the society we live in. If we can educate one person, it is an act of responsibility.

Ninth, sense of belonging. We belong to God and the church. The sense of belonging is very important to our lives. Without a sense of belonging, it is very difficult to progress in life.

Tenth, progress. We want to progress in many things, especially in education. But most important is spiritual progress. By doing this, giving a fistful of rice every time we cook, not only we contribute to the progress of the society and humanity but our spiritual progress.

Dear son, these are the benefits I am enumerating, but there are many more. There is a saying, a drop makes an ocean. By giving and setting aside this fistful of rice every time we cook, the church had established several schools in this land.

I had been a pioneering teacher in two schools before this present one here, in Ageville. I am getting my salary and feeding my family from the giving of a fistful of rice."

Then my father concluded, "Son, every time you give that fistful of rice, remember all these lessons I told you. But the most important thing is an act of Love for God. Tell this to your children and your grandchildren. Let them know these beautiful lessons of giving. Giving a fistful of rice to God through the church has many blessings to the person who gives and also to the society we live in.

There are many people with creative minds and novel ideas. These people persevered with these creative ideas and changed the world. Therefore, be creative, be innovative. And remember, collective efforts are very important. A small thing becomes big if you do it collectively."

13

Alone in the Wilderness of Life

IF YOU ARE IN the wilderness of life, climb up above. From there, you can get the clearer view, the better picture and see the larger horizon of life.

We came back from our work at the farm tired and hungry. I prepared food while my father checked his double-barrel gun. That was odd, because my father would always check the gun in the morning and never at night.

We had our simple but tasty food while the kerosene lamp shone in our small but beautiful hut. After the meal, I cleaned the plates, utensils, and all that needed to be cleansed. My parents had taught me to do this since a young age.

We rested after I had finished all the chores around the house. Before we went to bed, I was hoping my father would keep me entertained by his stories. However, to my surprise, instead of telling stories, he said,

"Son, let us go hunting tonight."

I was happy beyond words. We have the gun, but we never went hunting together. Sometimes he would allow me to carry the gun, but when he did so, he would take away the bullets. He did this to guide and protect me. Tonight would be an adventure of a lifetime.

The moonlight enveloped the entire night sky when we started from home. Millions of stars shone in the clear sky. I had with me the local machete while my father had a gun and his machete. We bolted the door of our house and left.

I was so excited to walk beside my father along the known village path. Then we reached the edge of the village and the forest grew thicker. We walk slowly, as we have to be careful. There were plenty of wild animals and many of these were dangerous.

After we had walked for an hour, my father left the usual path but ventured into the forest with no more identifiable pathway. When we walked in the thick forest, my father walked in front while I followed him. This was uncharted territory.

We reached a spot where my father found something, a kind of animal poop. He then signalled for me to stop talking. The wild animals were very sensitive to human scent and voices. He crushed this dry animal poop, scattered some in our clothes and put some of it in his bag.

We walked for another hour. We walked slowly, as if weighing every step. I held the machete in my hand while my father had a gun ready to shoot if any wild animal crossed our path.

Then we reached the top of one small, beautiful hill in the middle of the forest. It was here that my father did the unthinkable. He selected one of the tallest trees at the top of this hill and challenged me to climb this tree.

As village boys, we know how to climb trees. It was not an easy climb, but I could manage. At about two third of the height of this tree, the branches grew in such a way that it would be comfortable to sit and rest.

Before climbing the tree, my father told me to take the machete with me. Then, he told me he would go hunting alone while leaving me to stay alone sitting and resting on the branches of this tall tree.

My father forbade me to climb down until he came back. He told me in a hush tone, if you climb down and walk, hunters might wrongly take you as a wild animal.

I did as I was told. I climbed up the tree. When I reached those branches, I cut some small branches and leaves. To kill the time, I put those smaller branches and leaves in such a beautiful way to enable me to sit and relax there comfortably.

My father left me alone and disappeared into the thick forest. The moonlight shone, but I could no longer see my father.

While I sat there alone, in the middle of the wilderness and thick forest, in the middle of nowhere, I experienced that unexplainable thrill beyond description. Words failed to describe the songs of the night. I listened to the music of screeching insects as if synchronized in a choir. The moonlight shone on top of the trees enabled me a clear view of the horizon.

I was a young teen then. I had read some famous poets like Keats, Wordsworth, Shakespeare and others, but none could describe the situation I was in. The calm, peaceful moonlit night. The gentle breeze blowing the leaves of trees as if whispering with envy for a fortunate young boy like me.

While I sat on those branches of a tall tree, comfortably, I was in another and completely different world. I was far away from any human beings, except my father who would be somewhere there.

People may think that I was in a dangerous place or situation, but this was the safest place I could be. No one can harm me. I felt as if I was in heaven and the angels sang the beautiful music of the forest.

I did not know how long I had sat there. We did not have a watch or a clock. And while I was daydreaming in the night about the beauty of the darkness and the wilderness, the forest and the creations of God, suddenly my father showed up.

He came and told me to climb down. I was about to argue with him to allow me to stay a little longer to admire the beauty of loneliness in the forest. But then I thought better and obeyed him.

While climbing down, I had to be careful. I had to shift the focus of my eyes from the beauty above to the branches and how to climb down to reach the ground. Once I touched my feet on the ground, all that beauty seen from above vanished. A new type of beauty in the wilderness's darkness and forest came.

When we walked back home, my father told me to walk in front while he walked from behind, but was close to me. On the way, monkeys, apes, orangutans and many wild animals were visible to us. On this moonlit night, we could clearly see apes swinging from branches to branches of trees.

I thought my father would shoot one of those wild animals, but he did not. After I could no longer control myself, I asked him to shoot those animals with his gun. He replied to me with just two words: no point.

We reached home after midnight. We prayed and then prepared to sleep. I was lying in the bed, with the mosquito net tied firmly, but I could not sleep. The excitement of the hunting trip and the beauty of the wilderness made me anxious and curious. Finally, I asked my father,

"Pa, why did you take me hunting and then leave me alone in the forest, that too at night?"

"Son, I want to give you important lessons from real life. Time will come when you will be all alone in the darkness, the wilderness and the forest of this life. The bad and hard times always happen.

When you are in such situations, spend little of your time on the ground, but climb up above. On the ground, you will see darkness, dangers, thorns, and no identifiable path and therefore, difficult to find your way around.

But once you climb up from such situations, you will see the clearer view and larger horizon of life. Remember to be brave, be courageous and be patient. Be comfortable in any branches and the leaves above on the tree of life. Admire the beauty from above.

Another lesson is that you are growing up. You are in your teens now. I want you to experience the beauty of the wilderness and forest, especially alone at night. Then I want to test your patience, courage and bravery by asking you to climb and sit alone on that tall tree.

If you had said no, do not leave me alone. I would have done so. But it seemed you enjoyed being left alone. I admire your courage and now I can treat you no longer as a child but as a man. You passed the test brilliantly."

"Why that tree?"

"I knew these forests well. I had chosen the best tree and the best position for you to see. In fact, I did not take you hunting but to teach you important lessons in life.

You might think that I left you alone, but in fact, I was just a stone's throw from you. I was watching and observing your every move. You also know that as your father, your safety and well-being is my priority."

I have to ask him one last question which I had always wanted to ask,

"Here in this village, I got a wild tortoise. I met and played hide and seek with the wild deer while I carried your gun without bullets. We have together fought the wild black bear, not with any weapon, but by shouting with words.

There are plenty of wild animals here. But all these years, we never got to eat any wild animal meat. It appears you never use your gun to shoot any animal.

Tonight, we were very close to those monkeys, apes, and orangutans. I requested you to shoot them, but you refused. I do not understand, Pa."

"I have a gun, but yes, I never use it. I am a mission school teacher and a Christian. It was my decision to live, not only by teaching and preaching words, but to lead by example.

To make a better world, we have to preserve the environment and wild animals. We have to learn how to respect the mother earth and all the beautiful creations of God.

Once, in the village durbar, they discussed going community hunting. That was the tradition here. Every year, in the winter, the grown up villagers would go hunting together as a group. It was a thrilling experience in my youth.

But as a teacher and a headman, I decided it had to stop. I threw my weight around not to do this. I explained to them the importance of how to preserve the environment and wild animals.

When I did this, I created enemies. The bull owner[1] was one of them. Community hunting was like religion to them. Blocking community hunting was like blocking worship. That was also the reason he trapped your mother and me to pay that exorbitant fine as revenge.

It pained my heart that people do not understand. We lost our life's savings. But in the end, it came out well. The bull owner was once rich and powerful, but he had to leave the village a pauper and a hopeless man.

But God blessed me by giving me an extra job as a manager with the timber merchant. I not only make up for the loss as a fine to the bull owner, but God blesses us many folds more.

Son, before we go to bed, always remember to live by the examples we set. Life can be tough, but make it a priority to climb higher when you are in the dark and in the wilderness of life. When you climb higher, you can see the stars and the larger horizon of life."

I was sleepy but with pride swelling in my heart, I said, "Yes, Pa."

Countless times, I was alone in the darkness, the wilderness and the deep forest of this life. There were also times when only darkness enveloped my life and there appeared to be no way out.

But what my father taught me that night served me in good stead. I tried to climb and rise above those storms, challenges, and problems of life. I tried to stay above and be comfortable with whatever I had then.

Only later in life, I found I cherished those bad and hard times that I was alone in the wilderness of life. Because those terrible times forced me to climb higher, enabled me to see the stars and the larger horizon of life. Those times I was alone in the wilderness and the dark forest of life were, in fact, the spices of my life.

And above all, I could overcome and be what I am today is because the Lord Himself has said, "I will never leave you nor forsake you."[2]

1. Written earlier
2. Heb.13:5

14

The Charcoal Burner's Sons

It does not matter how humble your beginning is. What matters is how you progress in life.

Along with my brother, we sat on top of the gigantic Boulder 100. We sat there, admiring the beauty of the valley below and the cliffs above the boulder. This was one of the best days of my life.

How can sitting on top of a gigantic rock be the best day of one's life? It is difficult to explain, but let me try.

Our father was a humble morning school teacher. He led a very simple life. His salary was meagre, but he sustained himself and his family by working on his field and doing other menial jobs.

Every winter holiday, he would come home and take me to his farm in this small village. He taught me how to work on the farm and learn many important things in life. He taught me the dignity of labor and to respect even the lowliest of jobs.

Around the paddy field our father had converted from a swamp, there were many trees. Some of these trees were big, and some were small. These trees blocked the sunshine to the paddy field.

Paddy needs a lot of sunshine. If the paddy does not get enough sunshine, it will grow tall but with less rice. It would also take a lot of time to ripen. The paddy would take up a bigger space but it would bear less rice. The farmers knew the value of sunshine and its power to the plants.

So, we cut down all the trees, big and small, which block the sunshine to our paddy field. For smaller trees, we used them as fire-woods. For bigger trees, we burned them to convert into charcoal.

To make charcoal was a tedious job. Each log had to be cut to equal length. Then we dug a pit with a size big enough to fit these logs. The logs had to be arranged neatly. There should not be any space or opening between logs so that no carbon escapes.

For any small space or opening, we filled them with loose soil or green leaves. We filled these tightly so that the carbon would not escape. If an excess amount of carbon escaped while burning, the wood would turn into ashes rather than charcoal. If that's the case, our work and efforts would be useless.

Once we finished putting the logs, we covered them with green leaves and soil. From below, my father made a hole to put the fire to burn these logs. Once the fire burned, we closed the opening and left everything.

When my father inspected the charcoal burning place, he knew the condition of the charcoal burning inside by just looking at the cover on the top. If the cover became too saggy or down, then he knew that the charcoal would be less or turn to ashes.

However, if the top was firm and a tiny amount of smoke came, then he knew his efforts would bear fruit. There was a distinct smell from the burning charcoal. At the right time, we took out the charcoal, which was now ready for use or for sale.

Every Saturday, we put the charcoal in the jute bags and carried them on our backs to sell in another village about a one-hour walk. My father would carry the bigger sack while I carried the smaller one.

One particular Saturday, we carried our sacks of charcoal to sell as usual. Halfway through the journey, there is this enormous Boulder 100. On the base of this giant boulder, people had constructed a traditional resting place.

We put our sacks of charcoal down and rested there for a while at this resting place. While we rested there, curiosity got the better of me. So, I asked my father why we call this huge rock the Boulder 100.

This is what he told me,

"On the face near the top of this boulder, there was the number 100. Now that number is no longer there. Nobody knows who wrote it or how it was there. To me, the name Boulder 100 signifies the hugeness of this rock."

"So, was there someone who climbed this huge rock?" I asked.

"No, I do not think so. As far as I know, it is impossible to climb it."

"Why is it impossible to climb?"

"This rock is gigantic. Its slopes are slippery and almost perpendicular. I believed that there were people who tried but they could not."

As a young boy, I could not accept no for an answer. So, I told my father,

"Pa, one day I will climb and sit at the top of this rock."

I never knew how I would climb the gigantic rock, but the words came out of my mouth. I just believed that it might be possible.

My father just smiled and said,

"Well, son, maybe one day."

"But you told me to believe in the power of our words."

"Yes, words have power. I hope one day it will become a reality and only then you will realise the genuine beauty."

With that, we continued on our journey, carrying charcoal sacks on our backs.

Fast forward over forty years later.

I received the news that the daughter of one of our relatives who stayed in Ageville died. I called my brother and together we went to attend the funeral.

We drove up to a certain point and then left our car. The road was there but not fit for my car. Therefore, we walked. The sky was absolutely clear. There were no clouds, and the scenery was too beautiful.

We walked along the slippery road, reminiscent of the old days. In the old days, the path was small and rugged, zigzagged and longer to walk along the cliffs and gorges of the hills. But now, there is this road that was yet to be completed.

Then we reached the place where the Boulder 100 protrudes. The under-constructed road is from the upper side next to this rock. As we were in a hurry to attend the funeral, we told ourselves we will climb the rock when we came back.

When we reached the village, we found it had changed completely. When we were young, there were only thatch huts, but now almost all the houses have tin roofs or corrugated iron sheets. There were even a few houses constructed of cement.

When the funeral was over, we came back. We reached the Boulder 100 at the ideal time in the evening, where the breeze and the visibility of the valley below were at its best

The climb to the top of Boulder 100 was very challenging, but somehow we could reach the top. We sat on top of the boulder, admiring the beauty of the scenery around which was beyond description.

While sitting there, I looked down at the sheer size of this enormous boulder. From the base of this boulder, where the old path and resting place lies, it would have been impossible to climb to the top of this boulder.

However, when they constructed the road, they dug the hills from above the boulder. They filled the gap between the road and this boulder with rocks and other materials. The road now lies in a position which made the climb to the top of the boulder possible.

While I sat there, I remembered what I told my father over forty years ago. I told my brother what we discussed with our father then. How our father told me it was impossible to climb to the top of this rock, but today we were sitting on top of it.

There, on the top of Boulder 100, we discussed our lives. My brother being there with me was not a coincidence. We both have come a long way from what we were before. When we considered our backgrounds, educational qualifications and other yardsticks of life, we had progressed well beyond our wildest dreams.

While sitting on the top of Boulder 100 and admiring the beauty all around, I realised that there are many lessons in life from this.

I read somewhere that people treated the job of burning charcoal as one of the lowest. In many countries, people frowned and looked down at the job of a charcoal burner. I was the son of a charcoal burner, and I was myself also a charcoal burner.

However, that inferior position had taught me a lot about a humble beginning and the path we travelled to reach where we are today. No matter where you were before, it is possible to climb higher and higher.

Then I could not help but think about the changes in this world. Once upon a time, we had to carry loads on our backs and trudge that narrow and difficult village path. But now there is this road which makes life easier.

I realized that someone saw the need to construct the road. Many people, organizations and the Government were involved in the planning and construction of this road. The construction of this road made it possible for us to climb to the top of Boulder 100.

That is the same with us. Many people and things are involved in shaping and making possible the life we are in today. I am grateful for my parents, my relatives, teachers and friends, my school, my college, many known and unknown people who are responsible and shaped me into the person I am today.

Then the lesson from the trees that blocked the sunshine to the paddy field. There were many trees, big and small, which blocked the sunshine and blessings of God to reach my heart. My father had made it possible for me to receive enough sunshine by cutting down those trees by his stories, examples and his life.

Now I realize the importance of rains and storms in my life because then I can understand the value of sunshine, the countless blessings of God. The sunshine from Heaven enables me to grow.

Last but not the least, my father had cut the logs to the right sizes, put them into the pit, and covered them properly. After everything was right, he set the fire to burn the logs. Because he did his best, these logs turned not into ashes, but into charcoal.

God, my Heavenly Father did the same with me. When everything was right, He kindled the fire inside my heart to burn, to produce the desire and the willingness and the power to climb and reach the top of Boulder 100 of life.

And the vision and clarity of the valleys and cliffs of life is more beautiful when viewed from the top of life's Boulder 100.

PART II ───────────────

The Roots

1

The gods of Wealth

As humans, we are *free to make choices to worship anything. It's important to make the right choice. Because it's terrible to have made the wrong choices.*

We came back from Ageville when it was time for me to enrol in a proper day school in my mother's village which has one of the best village schools in those days.

We stayed in this beautiful thatched roof hut for a few years until our parents could save enough money to construct another, bigger house for us. It was in this beautiful hut that my younger brother and I, as children, learned from our parents many wonderful experiences of life.

The thatched hut we lived in was so beautiful inside and out. Our father knew how to make the house exquisite. But what was most important was the beauty inside. The joy, thrill, and happiness of childhood days remained with us, even to this day. Those days shaped our future.

Our parents were not only wise, but they were the best parents. Both of them are devout Christians and teach us many wonderful lessons of life. They not only taught us, but lived by those ideals. We are what we are today because of them. There were so many beautiful stories and lessons that they taught us.

The way our parents related those stories, sometimes we laughed, sometimes we cried and many other times we just listened to learn our lessons in life. This was one of those stories that remained etched in my memory and enabled me to change my life in many crunch situations.

We sat around the warm hearth while the small kerosene lamp shone its light on us. The fire slowly burned, while our mother narrated this wonderful story about how her parents became Christians.

Her grandparents and the entire family wanted to be rich and powerful. They knew that if they were rich, they would also be powerful. This desire consumed them. They wanted to be the richest people in the village. They wanted to control those around them and to get the respect from everybody.

They were well off by the standard of the village. But what they had was not enough. They wanted more. They wanted not only more but immense wealth and that too as early as possible. Then suddenly, they got this strange, baffling idea that they could become rich by approaching the gods of wealth.

How to approach the gods of wealth?

The eldest brother told them they could not approach the gods directly but indirectly. The gods of wealth would bless them and make them rich if they made sacrifices. They have to sacrifice animals, such as goats and cocks, to please these gods.

Being the eldest in the family, they obeyed him. They arranged for him to make the sacrifices. He did just that.

And the amazing thing was that it worked. They became rich by the standard of the village they lived in. All that they did was successful, and they became richer and richer. It thrilled them as they controlled the village and got the respect they wanted. They were the most powerful family in the village.

However, their power and happiness did not last long.

The eldest brother who made all those sacrifices died. The death was an enormous loss, but the bigger problem was that he never taught the rest of them how to make those sacrifices. Now, nobody in the family knew the system and ways to sacrifice to these gods of wealth. Since they do not have the know-how, they stopped making the sacrifices.

After they stopped making the sacrifices, members of the family started suffering from strange diseases. Strange things began happening in the family. They were rich and powerful, but they lived in perpetual fear.

Then the worst thing was that one by one of them died after suffering terrible illnesses. To witness the terrible sufferings of their loved ones was dreadful.

When they saw the terrible sufferings, and then the death of their dear loved ones terrified the family. They did not know what would happen next. Nobody knew who would be the next to suffer and die.

Then what they were most afraid of happened, the death of the grandmother. She suffered a horrible illness that tormented her. At last she died a terrible death.

After this horrible death of the grandmother, there was a family discussion, that being a practice in those days. They asked for divination from the people they consider knowledgeable about these things.

These diviners, after they have made certain animal sacrifices and calculations, all of them told that these gods of wealth were unhappy and angry with them.

The gods were angry and punished them because they no longer received the sacrifices and devotion required by them. Our mother's parents were afraid when they heard this. They realized now that they no longer knew how to satisfy and please these gods.

These diviners told them that if they could not sacrifice to feed and satisfy these gods, they would suffer terribly. They would eventually face an untimely death. Therefore, the family should find ways and means to satisfy these gods.

But how can they satisfy these gods?

Our mother's parents no longer knew the way or system to do so. They had to find a way or system to satisfy these gods, as the gods would stop at nothing until they pleased them. These diviners told them that to satisfy these gods; probably they needed human lives. What they were most afraid of was true. The family had to make human sacrifices.

That realization was dreadful to them. They could not do it, they would never do it. They have to get out of this deadly situation. At last, they consulted the Raja's sister (Local king's sister). It was a tradition in those days to do that. People believed that the Raja and his family could help those people who faced these situations.

The Raja's sister told them that the only way to save themselves was to leave everything. They have to abandon all their possessions, belongings, material wealth, and also system and beliefs. No more attachment with the old things that belonged to them. Leave everything and start a new life. That way, these gods would also leave them.

Therefore, to avoid being pursued and punished by these angry gods of wealth, they left everything. They left their house, landed properties, gold, silver, jewelry, costly traditional dresses and adornments, and all their belongings. The family fled empty-handed, with only the clothes they wore. They fled their old village and came to this village we are living in now to start a new life.

It was here in this new village, starting from scratch, they slowly and gradually built up their life. A few years later, before our mother was born, they converted to Christianity and accepted Jesus as their Savior.

It was in this village that I grew up. My grandfather passed away before I was born. Our grandmother passed away a committed Christian in good old age. I still remember her always smiling and beautiful face.

Jesus saved the family from the gods of wealth and blessed us. Today, we are a comparatively well-to-do and respected large Christian family in the village. Many of us had left the village because of marriage, jobs, and many other reasons, but we have not abandoned the faith.

What happened to our grandmother and her family, maybe over a hundred years ago, is also happening now. Many people wanted to be rich and powerful. They wanted to get rich and famous fast. Most of them could not wait.

Therefore, they would do anything and go to any length to achieve it. They would make all the sacrifices to the gods of wealth—time, health, family, children, belief system, everything.

And the amazing thing was that once we made those sacrifices, we would get what we wanted. But at what costs? If we count the costs, the result was alarming.

Our grandmother saw the sufferings, terrible death of her dear and loved ones. If we sacrifice to the gods of wealth, we will see sufferings, terrible physical and spiritual death of our dear and loved ones.

Our grandmother and her family left their old village, the old house, the old life, and everything old to save their lives and that of their children. At the beginning, they suffered, but God blessed them and they prospered spiritually and materially.

In the conundrum of living this life, many times I forgot this story told to us as children long ago. However, deep in my subconscious mind, it is always there. It has helped me countless times. But notable amongst them is the following.

There was a time when I made many sacrifices to get these material things from this world. Because of these sacrifices, I got a good and well-paying job in the bank. With my background, it was the best I could ever hope for.

I worked hard and loved the challenges. I got what I wanted to get. There was a time when I enjoyed those things. But at what costs? What my mother told us that night made me realize and calculated the debits and credits of life.

When I made a careful analysis, I found the debits were more than the credits. The tally in the accounts of my book of life was in the debit balance, or simply said, in the red. The gods of wealth almost took control of my life.

I had to leave these gods and idols of this material world and turn back the tally in the accounts of my life from red to blue. I must leave the gods and idols of this world and turn my life to the one and true God.

Can I really leave?

At fifty-three, I made a decision. I would not leave my belief system in the God of the Bible, my health, my children and family, and many of those real genuine important things of life for the sake of material and superficial things, like money, fame and position.

I took voluntary retirement from a senior management position at the bank to do the things I love, to live and enjoy a simple, happy, fulfilled life. I struggled at first, but now I found this was one of the best decisions I ever made.

Instead of bowing down and sacrificing my life to the gods of wealth, I now serve the one and only living God. And life is now beautiful and meaningful for me.

2

They Met Through the Bible

You lost something valuable. You pray, got it back and much more.

"Life is a miracle. Things that happen throughout my life are some sort of miracle. I thought I would never marry and remain a spinster, but God's plan and my plans are totally different."

This is what our mother told us when we asked her how she met our father.

"Why is that?" We asked.

"Because of several reasons. Right from my childhood till today, unexpected things happen. A few of those things are bad, but countless things are good and many are beyond my expectation. There were and still are moments when comprehending life's intricacies feels too hard.

However, regarding your question, let me tell you about myself. First, I am not a very healthy person. Second, I had passed a prime marrying age. Most of the girls in our villages are married in their twenties or earlier, while I was around thirty-five.

As long as I can remember, I tried to spend time reading the Bible and religious books. I love attending churches and fellowships. I thought I would spend my life this way, that I have no time for men. Maybe men were afraid of approaching me because of my age and religious leanings. However, God had other plans for me."

"But please tell us how you met and married our father."

As children, we were curious and more interested in knowing their love story.

What she shared with us that evening, as we sat around the hearth in our small but beautiful thatched hut, would always stay with me. People have told, and I have heard many love stories. I have also read many beautiful and well-written love stories. Some of them were like fairy tales. However, our parents' love story, to me, is the most wonderful love story and a romantic miracle that has ever happened.

We were young then, but what she told us was beyond words to describe. Now that I am a grown-up, I have read hundreds of books, but I have never come across such an amazing love story. It is not a fiction or an imagination of any brilliant mind, but it is true.

Our mother was born after the great-war (World War I). She is the fourth, in the large family of seven siblings of one brother and six sisters. As a child, she was told the story of how her parents left their old village.

They fled empty-handed from the wrath of the gods of wealth and later became Christians and accepted Jesus as their Savior. This had an enormous impact on her life. As she grew older, she became more and more religious.

She attended morning school just for a few years, but she was a good learner. They have the biggest house in the village—a two-storied building, a rarity in those days. Therefore, their house was the centre of social and religious activities in the village.

Therefore, while growing up, she was associated with church leaders and pastors. These leaders affected her personal life and worldview. She was more forward-thinking than most of her peers in those days. She was tall, slim, and beautiful with a wonderful voice. People admired her sweet voice when she sang.

Because of these qualities, the church frequently selected her to represent at many fellowships and church meetings. She travelled to many places to attend church meetings and gatherings. Despite her frail health, she enjoyed these occasions to see new things and learn new lessons in her life as a Christian.

When she was in her late-thirties, the church selected her as a delegate to attend the presbytery in another church at a village about three hours' women's walk. The journey required them to trek through the picturesque ravines and cliffs flanking the river.

She had been a veteran in walking like this, as she had attended many such church meetings before. Many times, she and her friends walked hundreds of miles on foot to attend church meetings.

The church hosting the presbytery selected the most qualified person to be the secretary of the church to organize this big event. The person selected was a mission morning schoolteacher, a widower with two sons. It was a historic occasion for their church, being the first time it held such a big event.

Everything was fine, except that on Sunday, after the night service was over, someone found a Bible left on the bench used by the delegates. They brought the Bible to the secretary. He opened the Bible and found the name and address of the owner written inside.

He tried searching for that woman who left the Bible, but it was late. The crowd had already dispersed, and the delegates had left to stay in their allotted houses, arranged by the host church.

The woman had forgotten about the Bible. They were happily chatting with friends and singing songs. They spent the last night of their stay in the house of their host by singing songs and hymns well past midnight.

The next morning on Monday, after breakfast, they packed their bags and left for their respective villages. After about three hours' walk, that woman reached home. Because she was too tired from the walk, she did not immediately open her bag.

Later in the evening, she unpacked her bag. It was then that she found out that her most prized possession—her Bible was not there. She frantically searched for the Bible, but it was not there.

She could not remember where she left it. Probably, she thought, she had left it in the church where she attended the presbytery. She could not go back to that village to search for her lost Bible. She prayed and hoped that whoever found her Bible would return it to her.

Meanwhile, the secretary of the church did everything in his capacity to find the owner of the Bible. However, later that day, they knew that the woman, the owner of the Bible, had already left for her village.

Someone from the church teased the secretary that the woman knew about him, a widower. Therefore, she intentionally left the Bible for him to find so that he would have to deliver the Bible back to her and marry her.

After making several inquiries, the secretary met a person who knew the woman's family. That person was originally from a village near the village of the woman who forgot the Bible.

Later on, this person told him that the woman was tall, beautiful, religious, and in her late thirties. He also told her she was single and was from a respectable family.

Those days there was no road, no telephone lines between these villages. Therefore, it was difficult to contact a person from one village to another, especially when that distance was about three hours' walk.

However, this did not deter the secretary from finding out ways to deliver the Bible. Through a series of events, the secretary of the church, along with that person who knew the woman's family, came to the woman's house to deliver the Bible.

On that fateful day, the secretary of the church, along with that person, came to the woman's house. After walking for hours, they reached the woman's house. The woman was eagerly waiting for them to receive back her beloved Bible.

After the traditional welcome, introduction, and formalities, the secretary opened his bag, took out the Bible, and handed it over to the woman. It was at this moment, with their eyes fixed on each other while handing and taking over the Bible, they fell in love.

She was now the happiest woman. She got back her prized possession, her beloved Bible. Not only did she get her Bible back, but she would also have another prized possession, her future husband. These were the two most valuable possessions any godly woman could wish to have.

Throughout their life, happy or sad, in joy or hardship, in health or sickness, whenever they looked at the Bible, their eyes glowed. When they read the Bible, it reminded them they did not know each other, but through this greatest book of love and salvation, they met. It strengthened them to go through life despite the many hardships and challenges they faced.

"My dear sons, what I wanted to tell and teach you is to always look at the bigger picture in life. There are always bigger things in life waiting for you. I forgot my Bible, but I got it back. The bigger thing was that through the Bible, I met your father, a godly man, and married him.

You should also know that this holy Bible has guided me in my entire life, has guided me to know God as it has guided me to meet your father. I faced many challenges in my life, but this Bible comforted me. So, when you grow up, let this greatest book, the Bible, be your guide in your life."

I knew from their stories and had witnessed the hardships and sufferings they had to go through. But they never wavered in their faith because they believed the Bible is the word of God.

This was one of the earliest memories I had about the countless stories our parents told us. Above all, what matters to us is that they instilled our young minds with a sense of wonder and belief. We believed the stories and words our parents told us. This also made us believe in unexpected and bigger things in life.

That is the legacy our parents left to us, me, and my brother. Through these stories, we learned many unique lessons in life. These stories and lessons helped us to navigate through the many unexpected and tricky paths of our lives. And the important lesson we learned from our parents is that they themselves read the Bible and tried their best to live by it.

Like my mother, I frequently forget about the Bible even after I've carefully placed it where it belongs. Yet, it was through the Bible she met our father. Likewise, I met and have fellowship with my Heavenly Father through this greatest book of all, the Bible.

3

The White Silk Turban

IF THE TURBAN FALLS, the dignity and honor falls. However, if the turban on the head remains intact and clean, the reputation of life remains intact and clean.

We sat around the hearth, in our thatched roof, modest, but beautiful home, happy to be with our parents. As usual, before Bible reading and prayer, our parents always tell us stories. Stories about their lives, their struggles and overcoming or from the Bible.

Tonight, my younger brother, who was around four years old, said, "Mei (Mother), please tell us stories."

I was around seven years old, three years older than my brother, and I interjected, "I think Pa (Father) can tell us a better story."

I did this because our father could make certain small things beautiful and always had something unique to teach us. His storytelling always had meaningful lessons for our life.

Our mother, smiling, nodding her head, agreed that our father could tell a better story.

We waited eagerly while our father took some time to increase our anticipation. Then finally, he told us this wonderful story about the White Silk Turban. This is what he told us.

It was a miracle when a certain man met a certain religious woman and fell in love. Their families were happy and planned for their wedding.

They arranged their wedding by following customary laws and Christian tradition. Then the wedding day came.

On this day, the bridegroom started from his village a bit early. They had to walk for over two hours on foot. At first, they traversed the plateau. Then they reached the deep ravine where a river flows in between these ravines and cliffs. The fore-fathers had made the path in a zigzag way, to make walking easier.

The groom started from home with his best man, and about twenty-five followers who make up the marriage party. In those days, it was only the males who went to the bride's house.

The wedding was a big celebration which normally you get only once in one's lifetime. However, for this groom, this was the second. Whatever the case, it was an important day for him.

The bridegroom, being a schoolteacher, could afford a costly dark blue suit. In those days, a turban was a must for a bridegroom as a mark of honor. This would show the respect, manliness, and dignity of the bride-groom. Therefore, apart from his new shoes, a costly new suit, he wore a costly new white silk turban.

Along the way, there were singing, shouting, and telling of jokes. Someone would sing out a phawar (a traditional rhyme in couplets, carrying deep, wonderful meanings). There was laughter and merriment along the way.

Then they reached the river. The Raja (Local king) had constructed a beautiful hanging bridge over this river to help the people cross it, especially during the monsoon flood. The scenery here was amongst the most beautiful.

On the western side of the riverbank, there was a gigantic slab of rock made beautiful by the erosion of millions of years. People who walk along this path always take some rest in this place. It was a customary resting place, as the walk was tiresome on both sides of the ravines.

They took a brief break to eat kwai (areca nut, betel leave, mixed with lime) and smoke pipes before crossing the hanging bridge and climbing the other side of the ravine. From here they walked the zigzag path and enjoyed the journey, continuing with jokes, singing, and phawar.

Just when they were about to reach the top of the plateau, there was a place that was wet because of monsoon rain, thick undergrowth, and not getting any sunlight to dry. This portion of the path was slippery and dangerous to walk on.

It was while they were negotiating, trying to cross this slippery patch of the path, that something unexpected happened. The bridegroom slipped and fell into the muddy patch below.

When the bridegroom fell, all were silent. It was a bad omen. When he stood up from where he fell, he found himself not hurt but dirty, wet and shocked. His shoes and clothes were wet and covered with dirt.

Looking at his condition, it was a miracle that his white silk turban did not fall. It remained fixated on his head. It was still clean, without a speck of dirt in it.

After the bridegroom recovered from the fall, all were tongue-tied. How could the bridegroom fall when all the members of the marriage party were fine and could easily cross the slippery path? The silence was so intense, you could hear a pin drop. Nobody spoke. The jokes stopped. Laughter ceased. All of them focussed on the bridegroom.

He started from home with the blessings of his beloved mother. Everything concerning his wedding from both sides was fine. So how could such an unfortunate accident happen?

Whatever the case, they could not go back. In whatever circumstances they were, they should proceed to the wedding. They proceeded ahead and reached the nearest river. In this river, the bridegroom washed his dirty shoes, socks, and suit.

It was here, after recovering from what had happened, that the elders in the marriage party discussed this unfortunate incident. Some of them saw it as a bad omen when a bridegroom slipped and fell on his way to the wedding. All agreed that something unpleasant would happen to him, his future, or the couple's married life.

This discussion happened while the bridegroom was trying to dry off the shoes, socks, and his clothes. This event and the predictions about the future had a profound impact on the bridegroom, leaving him extremely disheartened. His first wife died and now his second marriage did not look good. He was a worried man.

Amidst this feeling of doom and the sad state of affairs, one of the oldest men in the marriage party, calling the bridegroom to his side, said,

"Do not worry, my brother. As far as I can see, accidents happen. To slip and fall is part of our life. No one will learn to walk without falling. We learned that as children. So, in your married life also, the path and the journey can be smooth, rough, up, down, zigzag, and sometimes slippery. That is part of life, brother."

All the members of the marriage party listened intently to this old man, whom they considered the wisest. Though not educated, he was well-known for his common sense and wisdom. Then, putting his right hand on the bridegroom's shoulder, he said,

"My dear brother; you fell there in the slippery path, but you did not sustain any injuries. We should thank God for that. What if you got hurt? What should we do then? If you have injured yourself, then we should be worried.

Now nothing of these bad things happened. We should be grateful and thank God for that. You did not sustain any serious injuries. That means you may have problems in your married life, but that is part of our life. Who does not have marital problems? All married couples have.

Even if your clothes get dirty, you can clean and dry them. You could also purchase new clothes. What is more important in life is a healthy body and spirit."

Then, on a more serious note, weighing each word, to the bridegroom in particular and to the group, he said,

"However, this is the part that really counts. Have you seen it, my friends? Despite the slip and fall, nothing serious happened. But the most wonderful part of the miracle, I would say. . ."

The old wise man paused and then, pointing his index finger at the bridegroom's head, he continued,

"His White Silk Turban did not fall from his head. Not only that, it was still clean, with no speck of dirt in it. So, whatever happens to your married life, brother, your honour, self-respect, character, and dignity will always remain intact.

Embracing your problems can enhance your experience and caution as you walk the slippery path of life. But one thing I am sure of is that in whatever circumstances you will be in life, you will hold your head high. So, do not worry, let us proceed to the wedding."

These words brought comfort to the bridegroom. He believed in what the old man said. These words encouraged him. Whatever happened, they had to move forward.

Meanwhile, the bride was eager and anxious. She was the first in the family to get married in a Christian way. She was waiting for the bell to toll so that she could proceed to the wedding venue.

The suit, shoes and socks of the bridegroom were still damp. There was no more time to dry them. The consolation was that the clothes were damp but not dirty. From the river, they walked and climbed one more hillock into a forest, then they reached the village.

They went to the school building. The church building was in another village, a little farther away. They have arranged for the wedding to take place in the village school building.

When the bell tolled, everybody in the bride's family was happy. The bride now proceeded to the wedding venue. It was here, inside the simple school building, that they took their marriage vows. . . . .till death do us part.

"Pa," I said, suspecting all along, "That bridegroom was you. Is it not?"

"Yes, son." He acknowledged with a smile.

"So, my dear sons," he said to us, "please remember that life is like that. In life's journey, there are all kinds of paths. There will be laughter, songs, many fun and good things. But when you walk through those slippery patches of life, you may slip, you may fall, and your clothes may get dirty.

But one thing you should remember, the turban on the head of your life, should never fall to the ground. Not only that, it should remain clean.

What I mean to say is whatever problems you may face in life, keep your honor, self-respect, character, and integrity with no stain. Keep holding your head high.

Before I left home that day, I wrapped the turban properly and tightly on my head. I did not know that I would fall on that slippery patch. But what I did properly in the morning helped me later on that journey. The turban did not fall. Please remember that whatever you do, do it properly. It will help you along the way on this journey of life."

While navigating life's path, I've encountered countless slippery patches and fallen multiple times. I'm amazed that I've suffered only very minor injuries in my life. Looking back, I knew God protects me from suffering any major injuries.

Whenever I fall, my outer suit, my shoes, and my socks were dirty and wet, but not torn out. Luckily, I have been able to wash and clean them. Many times, my spirit was damp, but I could proceed ahead on my journey of life.

Many times, while traversing through life, I thought I was a hero walking to claim the love of my life. But many times, I found out I was a fallen hero. Despite being a fallen hero multiple times, I proceeded ahead to meet and claim those precious things I love in my life. It's a wonder the white turban of my character and integrity are still intact and clean.

Countless times, I forgot what our father told us that night. However, deep in my heart and somewhere in my subconscious mind, it remained. This helped and enabled me to rise each time I fall and move forward and keep holding my head high.

I had fallen, but what King David said was true, "Though he falls, he shall not be utterly cast down; For the Lord upholds him with His hand." Ps.37:24

4

No Place to Bury Their Dead Son

IT WAS NOT THE question of availability of land. It was a question of faith.

I am the eldest son in the family and my younger brother calls me "Bahbah", meaning elder brother. Why do my parents, my relatives, and other people call me "Bahrit" or "small brother"?

At first, I thought that since my father had two sons from his first marriage, they call me "small brother" to differentiate between them and me. However, I was curious to know the real reason my parents gave me this nickname.

Therefore, one night, while sitting around the hearth in our small beautiful home, I asked my parents about the reason they gave me this nickname.

I was stunned when, instead of answering, our mother's body language suddenly changed. Her face became pale and tears started flowing down her cheeks. I knew then that something deep had happened, and my nickname had something to do with it.

When we saw our mother cry, we hugged her. We love our parents so much and we did not want to hurt or make them cry. However, this made me curious, and I wanted to know the truth.

Then, our father raised his right hand to hush up. When I looked at him, I knew he would tell us the entire story, but waited until our mother recovered. What our parents told us that night was beyond description by mere words.

Our parents had told us many stories about their lives, their struggles, their problems, but this one truly touched my heart and had a tremendous impact on my life. While telling the story, my mother, me, and my younger brother cried. This is what our father told us.

The school he was teaching in Rabja[1] slowly and gradually grew. It was also during this time when our father got married to our mother. They met through the Bible and fell in love.

After marriage, our mother agreed to leave her village to stay with our father in that remote village. The distance from our mother's village to Rabja was about three hours' walk. So, our mother left everything she loved and cared for, her village, her family, her relatives, her friends, her church to follow her husband to a far, remote unknown village where he worked as a humble morning mission school teacher.

It was in this village that she became a wife, a teacher, a counsellor and suffered the worst time of her life. There they lived in a shed made for keeping potatoes and haystacks, provided by the family who donated the land to build the school.

On some occasions, when our father had to go out for other work, our mother would take over the teaching job. When I went there, the people of the village told me that our mother was a much better teacher than our father.

Her wisdom, sweet voice, and good handwriting earned her praise. Students, especially girls, preferred our mother to teach them than our father, so they told me. They told me that our mother not only taught them how to read, write, and count, but more about character, cleanliness, and hygiene, especially for girls.

It was during this time that our mother got pregnant with her first child. As she was not a healthy person even in her younger days, this pregnancy aggravated her health. Now that she was pregnant, she could no longer walk the three hours to go back to her mother's home. It compelled her to stay in the village despite her health conditions.

Our father was very concerned, but there was no other way they could do except to stay put in the village. It was in such circumstances that they committed their lives and prayed to God.

---

1. Name changed

With great difficulty, sickness, and pain, our mother gave birth to her first son. However, the worst part was that he died immediately after birth. Now, the couple in a remote village, far away from their relatives and friends, have lost their new-born son.

The way our father narrated the story made all of us cry. The light from the kerosene lamp shone and danced as if it listened to the sad story of the family. Our father told us he lost his first wife to death, and now his new-born son in this remote village in the middle of nowhere.

With his eyes swelling, as if looking at a distant strange world, our father told us that these were not the only problems they faced. While our mother was hovering between life and death, there was no outside help. There was no doctor, no nurse, or medicines.

He looked at his ailing wife, but he could do nothing to help or to ease her pain. The only thing he could do was pray to God.

To add salt to the injury, our father could not get a place to bury the mortal remains of their new-born son. There was no burial ground or cemetery. As the village was still following their traditions, they cremated their dead.

Those who opposed the opening of the school took this as their opportunity to show their power. Those few people tried to take advantage of this sad situation and opposed the burial of the dead body in the jurisdiction of their village.

To our father, here was his ailing wife hovering between life and death. Here was the dead body of his new-born son, but no place to bury him. Where should he turn for help? It seemed as if the universe had collapsed upon him.

When our mother knew her son had died, she was heartbroken, and tears flowed from her eyes. She could not even sit down in her bed. Our father held her hands and comforted her while inside his heart he was fighting a war that no one could see.

Meanwhile, our father sent a message to his relatives in his village about a one-hour walk away. They came right away.

Later, our father could send messengers to our mother's village to inform her relatives. There was no other way to send messages except that persons have to go personally to deliver the message. It took them almost six hours to walk both ways.

After they got the information, our mother's relatives came right away. They were aghast when they saw our sick mother and the dead baby. Our mother was lying in her bed, not able even to talk. All cried to see the sufferings our mother endured, especially when they learned that there was no place to bury the dead baby.

There was gloom in the shed our parents called their home. Some relatives used angry words, while some showed sadness, anguish, dismay, pain to see the situation our parents were in.

Amid hopelessness and despair, God would not let down the good people like my parents. Humanly, it may not be possible, but God miraculously answered the prayers of our parents and our relatives.

No matter the situation, there are always good people in this world. After some hesitation, those good people of the village rallied around our father. The good works our parents did had transformed the village.

Their children could now read, write, and count. Not only that, but they changed their manners, etiquette, vulgar language, cleanliness, and many other good things in life. There were positive changes in their lives.

On the request and negotiation from our father and relatives, the family that gave a plot of land to build a school, a shed for them to stay, pitied our parents. They donated the land large enough for them to bury the dead baby.

Now he got the land to bury his dead son but, what about the opposition for the burial? Meanwhile, the faction that wanted for the establishment of the school and sent their children to school impressed upon the opposition faction to allow for the burial.

There was a miracle. God worked wonders. Those who opposed the burial changed their hearts. They would not attend the burial, but they would not oppose it.

After many uncertainties, now our parents could bury their son. The entire faction who sent their children to school came to attend the burial of this baby boy.

Therefore, the body of the new-born baby, the first son of my mother, the third son of my father, and my eldest brother, was the first to be buried in the history of this village. They buried him on a beautiful hilltop to the west of the village.

"Son," our father said, "that is why we give a nickname and call you 'Bahrit' (younger or small brother) as a mark of respect and remembrance to our son who was buried in an unmarked grave in that far remote village, Rabja."

I visited this village a few times. I had walked the path my parents had walked before, a few times. Now this village is approachable by road. I had again visited this village a few times by car.

On one occasion, I met one of the oldest women in the village and talked with her about my parents. She was the first batch of students my parents taught. She had only good things to say about my parents.

I had also taken the help of village elders to show me the place where they buried my elder brother, but no one could identify the exact location of the grave.

Standing at the top of this beautiful hill, where my elder brother's mortal remains lay in an unmarked grave, I couldn't stop thinking. In this world, there are many types of people. In the long term, good people prevail. Good work always pays. Our father used to say, if you are good, even bad people are good.

My parents had taught me that when problems come, they come in a horde. There would be times where it appeared all doors of help closed. In such times, pray. If you look around, you would see only problems, but when you look up, God is there and opens those closed doors.

The sun had almost set, casting a light shadow on the entire village making the village enchantingly beautiful. I could not stop the tears flowing from my eyes when I knew and realized the hardships, problems, and sufferings my parents went through to do the things they love to do and contribute something to make this world a better place.

5

An Ambulance Chair for Our Mother

SHE LONGED TO GO back home. Despite her being sick, weak and unable to walk, they have to find a way for her to reach home

After the funeral was over, there was another unimaginable problem for our parents. Our mother was sick and needed special medical care. It was impossible to have any medical treatment or good care in this remote backward village.

Therefore, the best way for our mother to survive this ordeal was to take her back to her parent's home. She herself pleaded and wanted to go home. All present there agreed that this was the best decision.

But how to take her?

Our mother was so sick and weak from childbirth. She was sick in her body and the death of her first son affected her mental strength as well. Therefore, it was impossible for her to walk. She had to be carried, but how to carry her?

There in the small shed they lived, our mother was lying in a wooden bed, so sick and weak. There, our father and our relatives discussed the ways and means of how to carry her.

Had it been a young child, they could carry her on the back of a person. But she is a grown-up woman, and it was impossible to carry her that way.

There was a suggestion to carry her in the 'khoh-kit-briew', a kind of traditional cone made of bamboo and made to carry a sick person. Long time ago, they used this khoh-kit-briew to carry high-ranking government officials on their official tour to remote areas where even the horse could not go.

But the problem was that nobody had any such khoh-kit-briew in the area. People in the area hardly used this type of cone.

Then they suggested using a wooden chair. Those present agreed that this was the best possible way to carry her. They would use the wooden chair for our mother to sit and then they would use the '*star*'- a head strap made of bamboo strips or cane. They would use this head strap to carry the chair while our mother would sit in the chair back to back. With her health condition, that would be the best way to carry our mother back to her village.

All agreed with this idea, but again, there was a problem. Our parents did not have any chairs. All their known friends in the village did not have a chair. The village was remote and backward, and they knew of no one having a chair. The villagers used various traditional tools to sit but no chair.

Our father's relatives have chairs, but it would take them two hours to walk back and forth to fetch the chair. Anyway, they sent two youths there to bring the chair.

After almost two hours, they came back with a chair. They were about to put our mother in the chair, but they found a problem. It was an armless chair.

It would be unsafe to carry a sick woman for a long distance with an armless chair. The proper chair to carry a sick person had to be a chair with arms. The armchair would protect the sick person from falling while trudging the dangerous up and down zigzag paths.

By this time, the sun had almost set. They believed it was unwise to start a journey with a sick person in the evening. If anything happened on the way during the night, it would be a big problem for all concerned. They should start the journey early in the morning.

That evening, they discussed how to get an armchair. Meanwhile, our father prayed a silent prayer to God to provide him with the answer to get over this problem.

While all were struggling with what to do, a miracle happened. The most prominent man in the village came to visit our parents. It was a social custom to visit the home of the bereaved family to comfort them.

This man had argued and fought with the leaders of the village to have a school. He understood the value of education and therefore he was the first to send his children to the mission morning school. He was also the one who influenced the opposing faction of the village to allow for the burial of the dead body.

That evening when he came to visit our parents, he learned of the dilemma of not having an armchair to carry our mother. He saw an armless chair they brought, but it was unsafe to carry a sick woman in such a chair for a long distance.

This man told our father that one week back, he had purchased two armchairs. Looking at the face of our sick mother lying in her bed, he said he would give one of these chairs to carry our mother back to her village.

That evening it-self, this generous man left for his home. He came back later, bringing with him the armchair. This armchair was a perfect tool to carry our sick mother.

Our father thanked God for this miracle he did not expect. A person had just purchased two armchairs and gave one to him for carrying his ailing wife back to her village. It was a godsend and a gift beyond measure.

Our father offered to pay this man for the cost of the armchair, but he would not accept it. What our parents had done for the village was big enough for him. He said how he could repay the good works our parents did. On behalf of the village and his behalf, he gave the armchair as a parting gift to our mother.

What most touched our father were the words he used, or rather, a prayer he prayed. Although he was not a Christian, he surprised our father and everyone present by blessing our mother with such powerful words.

Our father told us that the traditional words and form of language he used were so deep and meaningful that you felt God listened to this prayer by a non-Christian. This was the best prayer our father had ever heard from a non-Christian.

Early the next morning, the entire village turned up to see this unheard of occasion of a woman being carried in an armchair. They also came to bid goodbye to our mother. There were no factions this time around; instead, everyone came together to bid farewell to our ailing mother.

While our father narrated this story, tears flowed from our mother's eyes. She wept for losing her new-born son, the sufferings she had to endure, but also because of the love and respect those simple villagers showered on her.

All the girls she taught came, kissed and hugged her. They also wept because their beloved teacher had to leave their village this way. These girls had learned many good things from her and it was an enormous loss for them. They wept to bid goodbye to our mother.

To carry our mother, our male relatives and many men from the village volunteered to carry her. The journey usually takes around three hours, but to carry a sick person, they had to walk slowly and carefully. They had to be careful while walking and negotiating through those dangerous zig-zag paths.

They put some clothes in the armchair to fashion as a cushion. That way, it would be comfortable for our mother to sit while being carried on the backs of other men. When the chair was ready, they conducted a small prayer service and then our father took our mother from her bed and put her in the chair.

Then they put the 'star', a head strap made from bamboo strips or cane, around the chair. The person who carried the chair put the head strap on his head and carried the chair on his back while our mother sat on the chair. They carried her this way until they reached her mother's house.

It was a long and tedious journey. Now and then, they would rest and take a turn to carry her. They started from Rabja early in the morning. They reached our grandmother's house in the afternoon.

Our grandmother was aghast when she saw the condition of our mother. Our aunt, our mother's youngest sister, who worked as a trained nurse, came along with the doctor. The doctor examined our mother and gave her the medicines.

Our mother recovered because of the medicines and also the proper and tender care from our grandmother. It was a miracle that our mother survived the ordeal, but our parents believed God had always been with them throughout.

I read this somewhere; I praise the genius who invented a chair, for without it we would probably be standing or just sitting on the floor. The chair truly is a simple tool that brings so much comfort to our daily life.

However, I would say that it not only brought comfort to us, but they used the chair as an ambulance to carry and brought our mother alive from death. Without that chair, it was difficult to guess what would happen to our mother.

Now we have ambulances with all life-saving gadgets to carry sick people. But there was a time, in this part of the world, when people used an armchair and other primitive tools as an ambulance to carry sick people. Our mother was lucky because, in some remote areas, even a chair was a rarity.

"Dear sons," our father finally said, "being carried on someone's back, as if being a child represented an act of humility and surrender. Pride and ego have no place here. Regardless of who you are or what you've achieved, there will come a time when someone will have to assist or carry you.

It is also an act of surrendering to the power of God. When sitting there on the chair while being carried by somebody, you know you are powerless. Even with no power from you, you knew you would reach your destination. Many times, life is like that. Even with no power from you, somehow you could reach the destination.

Sons, you may think that the armchair was the most important part of this episode, but it was not. A chair is only a tool for our use. If that man did not give us the chair, I would get it somehow.

But the most important things that last forever are the genuine love, the authentic respect, and the deep affection those simple folks gave your mother and me. That fervent prayer to God for your mother by a non-Christian man was solemn and heart-touching.

Those acts of love are the things which are important in life and sustain us in this journey of life despite the sufferings and pains."

6

270 Nights of Prayer or More

NEVER UNDERESTIMATE THE POWER of prayer! There is nothing impossible with God.

Our father had to decide between taking care of his ailing wife and teaching in the mission morning school he had started at Rabja. The school had progressed well, and he loved his job and the challenges of teaching his students.

The number of students had increased during these few years. Our father strived that all the children in the village should be able to learn how to read, write, count and be better persons in life.

He also loved his wife. Her mother and all the close relatives had taken excellent care of her at home. The medicines she took and the care she got were the best he could expect in those days. However, as a husband, he knew it was his duty to be near his ailing wife.

Therefore, it was difficult for him to decide. He loved his job, and he also loved his wife. Initially, he tried to serve both. Could he serve two masters?

On Monday morning, he would wake up at four o'clock. He then would start his journey from his mother-in-law's house at four thirty in the morning and walk for three hours to reach Rabja. He would open the school at seven thirty in the morning.

After the school was over, at about ten thirty, he would walk again for three hours to come back to our mother's village. He walked six hours each day to serve his job as a schoolteacher and to be near his wife. It was fine for a few weeks, but it was impractical in the long run.

Then he started on Monday morning and stayed back at Rabja. At ten thirty on Tuesday, he would come back by walking another three hours to be with his ailing wife. So, he would stay in Rabja for alternate days. Again, for a few weeks it was fine, but then walking eighteen hours every week to serve his wife and his job was again too difficult.

He did this for over a year, facing storms, rains, and good days. But he found out that it was impractical. The salary he got was meagre. He used to sustain himself and his wife by doing extra odd jobs or working in the fields for agriculture. However, he was using his extra time for walking instead of being productive.

It was impossible for his wife to go back and stay with him in Rabja. Even if she was willing, her relatives, especially her mother, would never allow her to do so. Therefore, after taking everything into consideration, he finally made a decision. With a heavy heart, he resigned from the job he loved, to be with his dear wife.

It was during this time that his wife became pregnant once again. In some cultures, they really took good care of a pregnant woman. I have read many stories about pregnancy and pregnant women, but what our father told us was beyond words.

I have tried to research to find such a thing but till date I could not find any record. Probably people did or might do it but I could not find any such record in writing.

To be a bearer of a new life is very exciting. That's the same with our mother. When she informed our father of the good news to our father, he was ecstatic. He looked forward to being a responsible father once again.

I have read some rituals that people across many cultures did when they learned about pregnancy. There were many things people did when they learned about the pregnancy. But what our parents did was something unique.

Our parents put so much importance on prayer. They made prayer a ritual in their daily life. It was not a surprise when they prayed that night. But their prayer that very night was not the usual prayer but a unique special prayer dedicated to that new soul being formed in the mother's womb.

When they retired to their room, sitting in the bed together, holding their hands, they bowed down in prayer. They started with the usual prayer, but especially they praised the Lord for this new blessing. They knew nothing about the science of spirituality,[1] but they consecrated that newly formed child inside the mother's womb to the Lord.

I imagined these two beautiful souls—my parents—praying fervently for that soul, their progeny being formed, blessed by the Lord to be their offspring. They kept behind them the memory of their first son who died, but looked forward to this gift of new life in their life together.

They were simple people, but they prayed to the Lord to give them wisdom to enable them to take proper care of the baby inside the womb until the birth. Our parents also prayed for the well-being of that baby after birth.

They knew their limitations, but that did not deter them from seeking the wisdom and guidance of God to be exemplary parents. Our parents prayed for that new soul and for themselves as well.

For 270 nights and probably more, they prayed continuously, every night. The winter nights were chilly, but they prayed. The warm summer nights were long, but they prayed. They worked hard and were tired, but they prayed. They had problems and challenges, but they prayed. Whatever the circumstances in their life, they prayed. They prayed for that yet to be born baby and for themselves.

The kerosene lamp was glowing its light on the stand when our father told us this story. The firewood was burning in the hearth, giving warmth to us and the entire house before we went to sleep. In the solemn atmosphere of the night, I asked my father why they had to pray so much for this kind of prayer.

Our father solemnly answered my question.

First, they suffered the trauma of losing their first son in Rabja. They did not want to lose this baby.

But why pray on the first day they knew about the pregnancy?

They consecrated the newly formed life of the yet to be born baby. It did not matter to them whether that baby would be a boy or a girl, but they trusted that to the Lord. Our parents wanted to consecrate the baby not after that baby was born, but right when the mother conceived.

Second, they prayed for the health of the baby inside the womb and for the health of the body and spirit after birth. That foetus inside the womb

---

1. The Spiritual Child by Lisa Miller, Ph.D.

was precious, and they needed to have the wisdom to know that it was a blessing from God. They wanted a bright future for that yet to be born baby.

Third, they prayed especially for themselves. They knew the problems of parenting. To guide their children properly, they needed wisdom right from the day the conception of the child started in the mother's womb.

Our father said that if you get the child right from the womb, you get their childhood. When you get their childhood, you get them when they grow up. But if you don't get them in their childhood; you don't get them when they grow up. Losing the children to the power of this world would be the worst nightmare for God-fearing parents.

Fourth, they dedicated that yet to be born baby, and themselves, to God. They knew the uncertainties of life and the faithfulness of God. They had experienced that themselves. Life is full of difficulties and problems, but they prayed for God to give them the resilience to overcome these challenges of life.

Fifth, by praying, they learned the importance of gratitude, faith, trust, wisdom, and, especially, for love. They prayed for the innate understanding of the sanctity of their family. They prayed that they and their children would have a close affinity with God. Our parents committed their life to do the best they could for themselves, their children, the society, the church and most of all, God.

I had gone through many phases in life: those thrills and happiness of childhood, the best of times with my brother and my parents. I had also gone through the problems of adolescence, and the difficult teenage years of rebellion.

We lost our beloved mother during the time I most needed her. I quarrelled and had a face-off with my father and later regretted it. I had many problems and challenges to continue my studies. But despite all odds, I graduated from college.

There were countless tears of rejections and disappointments. Oh! I have tasted the joy of overcoming and success. The excitement of getting married and the challenges of married life. The thrills and problems of raising children.

It was wonderful to serve the Lord, but anguish when I fell down into the pit of destruction. I have abstained from committing sin but had fallen into temptations. Endless times, I have tried to become the best person, but I also have a streak of madness.

I have endured patches of sickness and pain, but have also enjoyed good health and joy. Many times I failed, but countless times I won. In short, I have suffered tears, sadness, despairs, and hopelessness. I have also tasted and cherished the success, love, respect, overcoming, and happiness.

Reflecting on my past, my life was quite extreme. The severity of the bad things that happened sometimes made life nearly unendurable. During those hard times, like Job, I complained and asked God why me?

However, those bad times, even if they seemed extreme, were always transient. Somehow, something beyond my understanding always happened. I experienced several miracles in my life that were unbelievable. When those good things happen, many times I feel as if I was in paradise or in another world.

But throughout this difficult and beautiful journey we called life, those special prayers by my parents for 270 nights or probably more sustained me. Those prayers served me well in all the circumstances of my life.

Why? Because the precious yet to be born child our parents fervently prayed for, right from the first day, when they knew about my mother's pregnancy, was none other than *"Me"*.

But what about my brother? He endured demonic epileptic seizures, tape worms, kidney stones, one damaged kidney removed, and various other afflictions.

My parents prayed the same prayers for him as well. Therefore, thanks to those special prayers by my parents, my brother could withstand those hard times and be cured from these afflictions. He is now living a fulfilling life.

7

The Pastor Gave the Name

WHAT'S IN A NAME? *Plenty.*

After the security and safety inside the mother's womb, the healthy baby boy was born to live and face his new world. Both the mother and the baby were doing well. All the relatives, especially the grandmother and the father, rejoiced on this occasion. They welcome this bundle of joy with prayers and celebrations.

The parents were relieved that God answered their prayer. The trauma of losing their son in Rabja and the sufferings they faced was now behind them. Now there was only joy and happiness at the birth of this healthy baby boy. The parents accepted this child as a gift from God.

After the celebration and joy, they have to give this baby a name. There were many suggestions from well-meaning friends and relatives. The father listened carefully to all these suggestions. However, deep in his heart, he knew the importance of giving a name to his son.

The father knew the name of his child would be the greatest connection to his own identity and individuality. Therefore, a name should be meaningful, showing the blessing of God, indicative of his life and future.

Amid all these, the father asked for suggestions from his wife. Probably, she would have something in her mind to name the precious child. People could give any name to their baby. There was no restriction according to traditions, as they were Christians.

Since there were many suggestions, the mother could not decide. Then she remembered her wonderful mother-in-law. Her mother-in-law loves and cares for her so much that she would do anything for her. Therefore, as a respect and honor to her, she told the father to let his mother, the paternal grandmother, name this boy.

That would be the best, since that was the tradition being followed by most people in the community. Although it was not compulsory, all agreed that this would be the best option.

Since his wife and son were doing fine, one week later, the father left for his village over two hours' men's walk to inform his mother. While walking the deep terrains and winding path, the father was extremely happy.

He had reluctantly left his job as a mission morning school teacher at Rabja. The birth of a son signifies a new beginning for him, his wife, and the baby boy. There is hope for the future of his family. He praised God for all the blessings showered on him and his wife.

It was a sunny, bright day. The scenery was extremely beautiful. Down below, midway from the village of his wife and his own, runs a beautiful river signifying the timelessness of God.

While walking, he thought about what name his mother would give to his new-born son. He wished and prayed that his beloved mother would give a suitable name, which his son would carry for a lifetime.

Suppose his mother could not give a satisfying name. What would he do? Could he suggest a name for her? If she asked for his suggestion, what name should he give? He was thinking of some biblical names. Then he thought that the best way was to first consult with his mother. Together, they would decide on the best name.

While thinking about the best name he could give his son with the consultation with his mother, he found he had reached the river. He was about to cross the beautiful hanging bridge constructed by the Raja (Local king) when he saw someone coming from the opposite direction of the path.

He was about to cross the hanging bridge when he realized that the person who came from the other side was his pastor. He was delighted to meet the pastor after a long time since he left his job and was staying in his wife's village. They shook hands.

They needed to talk. There was so much to talk about. They have so much to tell each other. There on the river bank, on the stone slab, made beautiful by erosion for millions of years, they sat down to talk. The clear crystal water flowed in the river while the fishes, big and small, swam gleefully. The majestic hanging bridge stood at the backdrop from where they sat down to talk.

After the greetings and salutation, they discussed those things they wanted to know and wanted to tell each other. The pastor knew the reason the father left his job, the death of his new-born son in Rabja, and the sickness of his wife. So, he asked about the health and condition of his wife.

There, both sitting on the beautiful big slab rock, the father proudly told his pastor about the most wonderful news that one week back, she gave birth to a healthy son. Both his wife and son were doing well.

The pastor then said,

"Have you given your son a name?"

"Not yet. I am going to my mother's house. I will consult with her to give a proper and suitable name for him."

Without batting an eyelid and with his firm pastor's voice, he said,

"Name him Kitbok."

While sitting there on the stone slab, on the river bank with a beautiful hanging bridge in the background, the pastor explained the meaning and significance of giving this name.

First, Kit means to carry on the back, like carrying your sick wife in the chair along these same winding paths. Your son would carry his parents in times of trouble or sickness. He would also carry forward the faith, dedication, the love, and other wonderful traits of his parents.

Second, Kit means to support, to prop, to hold on. Your son would support you, your wife, and his siblings. He could act as a prop that you can lean on. In times of troubles, he would be the support that you could hold on to for life.

Third, Kit means to bear. In those difficult times, your son can bear the heavy burdens of life and forge ahead. I pray your son will bear good fruits and many greater things in life.

Finally, Kit also means to endure or endurance. He could endure anything or until he overcomes. Life is tough, but endurance is the quality God would endow your son.

Like this beautiful hanging bridge, pointing his finger at the hanging bridge, which endures all weathers and the weight of people crossing it, your son will also be able to endure many things. Both of you as parents have endured sufferings but the son could also endure whatever he has to go through in life.

Then the pastor explained the word 'bok' means- luck, lucky, fortune, or fortunate.

To emphasise the points, he explained, luck and good fortune would follow your son. Not only in material things, but especially in those genuine important things in life.

Your son needs all the luck and good fortune to thrive in this life. For example, when the father leaves for the journey before he starts he would ask the children to put their palms in his palms as a sign of good luck. Whatever happens to his future, we expect good things out of him.

Last but not the least, it denotes fighting, just like a clenched fist. In the battles of this life, like a boxer, your son would not surrender without a tough fight.

Now you combine these two words, Kit-bok, you get a pleasant sound to the ear, simple to understand, powerful with deep meaning, and indicative of the future of the boy.

Finally, the pastor said, "I am a pastor and there is something deep inside my heart which tells me to give you this name. Therefore, please name him Kitbok."

With that, they talked about other important things that happened to them. About half an hour later, after a prayer and special blessing to the yet to be baptized baby boy, Kitbok, by the pastor, they parted ways. Both of them walked in the opposite direction, climbing the slopes of the beautiful cliffs and terrains along the winding path.

The father walked the winding zigzag path to his mother's house, deep in thought. What happened and what the pastor told him was beyond his comprehension. Was it a coincidence or a godsend?

When he reached his mother's house, he told her everything. The birth of his son and especially the meeting with the pastor at the bank of the river midway between the two villages. He told her everything, leaving nothing.

Then the father asked his mother about her opinion.

His mother said, "His name shall be Kitbok. I agree with what the pastor said."

When our father told our mother about what happened, our mother agreed to name the child that is me, Kitbok. Deep in her mind, she thought about her sufferings at Rabja, the prayers, and her firm belief and faith in the power of God. What would happen if what the pastor told came true? She committed everything to the mighty hands of God.

Part II: The Roots

We are from the Presbyterian denomination, and they baptized the children when they were young. Yet, for multiple reasons, my parents got me baptized when I was over six. I still remember how the Pastor held my head and pronounced, "Kitbok, I baptized you in the name of God the Father, Jesus Christ the Son and The Holy Spirit, Amen."

When good things happened, many times, I forgot about what the pastor told my father. However, when I had to walk those dark valleys in this journey of life, the words the pastor told my father enabled me to go forward. Those words spoken by the pastor when I was about one week old are still reverberating in my ears today.

Frankly, I do not deserve what the pastor told my father, nor the faith my parents had in me. But along the way, I have a fair share of what the pastor told my father. I learned many lessons from those struggles and problems I faced to live a better life. I cherished those good things, which are countless, to make this life meaningful.

Life is too deep to describe in words. From inside the womb of my mother, throughout my life, and probably till my last breath, deep wonderful and miraculous things happened and keeps on happening in my life.

PART III

On The Slope of a Hill

1 ————————————————

Three Snakes Crossed
and Blocked Our Path

Many menacing, sinister, and ugly things hamper our progress in life. We need fortitude, wisdom, and patience to overcome these alarming obstacles.

Our parents had saved enough money and built a CGI roofed bigger house on the slope of a beautiful hill. We were so proud to have got a bigger house and we shifted from our old thatched house to this house. We had the best of times and the worst of times in this house.

We encounter odd and bizarre experiences countless times in life. It was hard for me to understand when these events occurred. When these things occurred in my life, I asked how and why such strange things happened to me.

Many times, it was challenging to comprehend the occurrence and timing, but only later did I have some idea about the purpose or meaning behind such things.

Here is an incident that was bizarre and strange, which happened while walking the path along with my father.

We went to my father's village for the wedding of his niece. We walked along the old path where strange and interesting things happened to us.

Our father slipped and fell down on his wedding day on this path. They carried our sick mother in a chair along this path. Our father met the pastor, who gave my name, Kitbok, here on this path. Many other things happened to us on this up and down zigzag path.

On the morning after the wedding, we set off from my father's ancestral village as the sun rose high above the sky, to come back home. Along the fertile fields, we walked for a few minutes. Beyond that lies the jungle, followed by a downward path along the gorges and cliffs to the river below.

My father carried with him his double-barrel gun. In our hands, we have our walking sticks for support and protection during our walk. I was a few steps ahead of my father as we walked.

Just a few minutes into the jungle, I saw a not-so-big brownish snake laying across and blocking our path. When I saw the snake blocking our path, I stopped.

When my father saw the snake blocking our path, he overtook me and used his walking stick to strike and kill the snake. He hit the snake's head several times to confirm its death.

He used the walking stick to remove the dead snake from the path and put it onto a boulder, ensuring that nobody would step on it. My father said that stepping on the dead snake with bare feet could cause poisoning from its bones for both humans and animals. Therefore, it was important to place the dead snake correctly to prevent anyone from trampling on it.

After this incident, I sensed my father's unhappiness through his body language. A snake obstructing the path, regardless of its size, was not a positive omen. However, we continued with our journey.

We reached the slab of rock near the river. On this beautiful resting rock, we sat down to rest for a while. While resting there, we also ate our lunch packs prepared by my father's relatives.

After lunch, we crossed the hanging bridge and continued on the upward zigzag path. Before the place where my father had his wedding day mishap, there was a small stream. Just as we were about to cross the stream, we saw a gigantic blackish snake slithering across our path.

When we first saw it, we could not see the head or the tail, except that it slithered downward, blocking our path. According to my father, it's estimated to be about twenty to twenty-five feet long.

There are no words to explain my fear. My hairs stood on their ends. In plain words, my experience was like being in hell, not here on this earth.

While the big black snake slithered downward, I signalled to my father to shoot it with his double-barrel gun. He signalled back by shaking his head.

We just held our walking sticks, ready for any eventuality. We were ready to fight in case the snake attacked us. However, the snake did not appear to care. It just crawled, taking its own sweet time, down the forested terrain.

While standing there together, my father and I lost track of time as we waited for the snake to disappear into the forested terrain below. Even after the big black snake disappeared, we just stood there, too shocked to continue on our path.

The experience I had that day was eerie and beyond description. I was lucky my father was there with me. If I had been alone, I would not know what to do.

When we realized that the big black snake had disappeared and there was no more danger for us, we continued on our journey onwards. To walk over a path where the big black snake had just crawled was surreal.

Once I regained my composure, I asked my father why he did not use his double-barrel gun to shoot the snake. He told me it's too risky to shoot a moving snake with a gun. Never forget, he told me, an injured snake is more dangerous than anything else.

After this, we continued on our journey without talking as we were too shocked from this strange encounter with the small brownish snake and the big black snake. The journey back home turned depressing.

We walked until we reached the river where our father washed his clothes on his wedding day. After that, we ascended one more forested hillock and then reached a small gravelled road.

As we continued walking, another spooky and shocking incident unfolded. A little distance ahead, another big greenish snake was crossing the path. Just like before, we couldn't see its head, only its body as it crawled across, blocking our path. The size of this greenish snake was almost the same as the blackish snake.

The shock for us was beyond words. The scene was nightmarish and unexplainable. We had a clear view of the snake, except its head was deep inside the forest. This big greenish snake crawled across the path from the western side to the eastern side of the forest.

It took us longer than expected to recover from the sudden appearance and crawling of this massive snake. The snake disappeared into the thick forest as we stood there, watching in silence. It was a horrifying experience that felt beyond this world.

When we recovered from the shock, my father examined the area for any dangers. Then, he pointed his finger to one place near a large tree, where we could sit.

While sitting there under the tree, my father explained these macabre incidents with a heavy heart. With a very serious tone, he said,

"Son, the first not-so-big brownish snake was just a part of our journey. If it had not blocked our path, we wouldn't have killed it. We did not set out on this journey intending to kill snakes or any animals.

We couldn't proceed by stepping or walking over the snake. If a snake lays or obstructs our route, we must kill it. Animals, whether wild or tamed, should not impede a person's path, journey, or progress.

But we had to halt our progress when we came across a second enormous black snake. You gestured for me to shoot, but it was too risky. If I shoot the snake, I should shoot it at its head. That would ensure its instant death.

But we did not see its head, which is good for us. If we saw its head, the snake would have also seen us. Then the snake might have reacted and attacked us. That would be bad for us.

Shooting the snake from any other parts of its body would be too dangerous. The snake may not die instantly, even if I hit it. The snake was massive, but there's a possibility I might miss it if I shoot it, because I am not a professional shooter. Therefore, shooting the snake would be too dangerous and suicidal for us.

However, for the third snake, it appears you are wiser. You weren't in a hurry, but you were waiting along with me. I saw you were ready with your walking stick for any eventualities. It is always better to be prepared in all kinds of situations."

While explaining to me, he reasoned that since both these two massive snakes showed no aggression towards us, there's no need to attack or harm them. He emphasized the importance of logical thinking and patience in dangerous situations, highlighting their importance over rash decisions and immediate reactions.

On a more serious note, he continued his insights with me,

"We don't know why we encountered three snakes on one journey. I do not know the reasons, but I have a hunch that the journey of life ahead of us would be very tough or challenging. I expect significant difficulties and hazards in the path of life ahead, which could become perilous if we were not careful.

We can eliminate or overcome those minor problems, such as that small snake. However, we have to be very careful with those big challenging problems ahead in our life. Guns and sticks won't work; we must practice patience and wait.

I believed in my heart that these were God's warnings for me to be cautious in life's journey. Son, you have witnessed those massive, fear-inducing snakes.

The welfare of our family and our future is most important to me. What we encountered today seemed too bizarre and dangerous, but nothing bad happened because we waited with patience and let things pass.

On every occasion, I prayed before doing anything. I sought God's guidance with a silent prayer. I prayed when I saw the not-so-big snake because snakes rarely block human paths.

Son, therefore, before we proceed ahead on this journey, let us pray. Prioritize prayer and thoughtful response over immediate reaction. In crunch situations, remember to be slow and steady because patience is bitter, but its fruits are sweet."

We closed our eyes and prayed, trusting God to protect and guide us in whatever circumstances we may face on our journey of life. Then we proceeded home.

Throughout these years, I learnt many lessons from this strange, unimaginable encounter and what my father told me that day. Some of these lessons are, one, to strike at the proper place or the source, to win or to immediately overcome those minor problems we encounter.

Two, it's important to put those problems in the right place to ensure others don't suffer from them.

Third, tough problems in life are unavoidable. Guns and sticks would not suffice or overcome these, but logical thinking and patience do. If you can strike the problems from its head or from the source to kill it, it would be fine.

Fourth, many times, it is impossible to know or see the head, the source, or the origin of these problems. Therefore, once the problem has already started, it is better to be patient and wait.

Fifth, then there was a time when I thought my father was foolish in his thoughts and actions, but later I found he was the wisest man who gave me the best he could—because what he taught me and what he had foreseen was more than true.

There were many other lessons, but I learned from these experiences that my father was there to do the best for me. But most important is that my Heavenly Father protects and guides me from the snakes of this world, big and small. I am what I am today because of His guidance and protection.

2

Epileptic Seizure or Demon Possessed

THERE ARE COUNTLESS QUESTIONS of life which there is no plausible answer. Only God knows

What our father had predicted and told me that fateful day we encountered those three snakes came true. He had foreseen the tough and challenging problems of life ahead of us.

It would be impossible to write all these problems, but let me tell you about some of them on these pages. And this was one of the scariest gigantic problems, I would say.

Our father had purchased one small young cow. At the beginning and at the look of it, it was a small and skinny cow. We discussed this with our father.

But our father, being a wise man and an expert on these, told us he got a good price for this cow. He had calculated the ratio of the length of its legs vis-à-vis its body and knew that the small cow would be a big one in due course if we took good care of it.

As guided and taught by our father, we took good care of this small cow. As predicted by him, it became a big one. Then our father sought the best bull for mating. We saw first-hand how the mating was done.

In due course, this cow gave birth to a female calf. Our father took this opportunity to teach us milking. It was fun to learn new things, but it was tedious to do it every day. However, it was this tedious job of milking that supported my schooling expenses and also for college. It was also the source of many good things and a few bad things later in life.

One summer Saturday afternoon, our father, I and my younger brother cleaned the cowshed and its enclosure. While cleaning the shed and the enclosure, we got dirtied. As our bathroom was small and we did not want to take a good bath inside the small bathroom.

Therefore, we suggested to our father that we could go to the nearby village river to bathe ourselves and also to wash our dirty clothes. Our father agreed.

After we finished cleaning the shed, the enclosure and its surrounding areas, all three of us went to this not-so-big but clean river to wash ourselves and also our clothes. As village boys, we knew how to swim and we took to water and swam like fishes. We enjoyed the evening thoroughly.

When we finished washing the dirty clothes and bathed ourselves, we came back home carrying with us the washed but wet clothes and wonderful memories.

That night, we milked the cow and had our dinner as usual. Then, as was our practice, we had our story telling times with our parents. We talked about many things concerning our education and our life ahead of us. Before going to bed, sitting around the fireplace and a small kerosene lamp, our father prayed our bedtime prayer.

It was in the middle of the prayer that something stranger than fiction and out of the blue happened. My brother suddenly convulsed and fell down from his seat. With no provocation, he had a terrible seizure and his whole body shook.

Our father continued his praying for sometimes but when he heard the commotion, he had to say Amen. When we opened our eyes, we witnessed a terrible scene. There were no words to describe what happened to my younger brother.

The sounds he uttered were spooky and incomprehensible. His body bent as if it was a plastic or a spring, and he writhed in extreme pain. He stuck out his tongue, and we tried our best to hold his mouth so that he would not bite or hurt his own tongue.

We did not know how much time this suffering continued because we did not have a watch, but it must be at least half an hour before my brother recovered. He was terribly weak from this suffering. We gave him water and took him to our bed for a complete rest.

When he had finally recovered, our father asked him to tell us about his pain and suffering during the epileptic seizure.

This is what he told us,

"While we were praying and closed our eyes, suddenly I was in the field very near the river we swam. There, the terrible-looking devils and demons came and fought with me. They were so strong and overpowered me. I was no match for them. Even then, I did my best and struggled and fought the hardest battle I ever fought.

While I was fighting, I heard the voice that someone shouted, Jesus, Jesus and these devils and demons tried their hardest to kill me. However, when that voice kept shouting Jesus, Jesus, these devils and demons became weaker and weaker. Later they left me alone and then I became conscious and realised I was at home with you."

When we asked him to explain the shapes and sizes of these devils and demons, he told us. It is impossible to explain in details what he saw but let me try:

These devils and demons were of varied shapes and sizes. Some of them were like horses, goats, snakes and many other shapes, but they were frightening to look at because they have terrible looking horns and teeth. Some of them have tails like the dragon wagging and ready to cut the human skin. They have horrific looking tongues sticking out to suck blood and are ready to eat human flesh.

At the beginning, we thought that this seizure was a one-time accidental occurrence. However, it kept on happening, especially when we wanted to make a family prayer. Then, as time passed, it became more frequent and more serious.

Every time he had his seizure, he would tell us about the strange fight between him and those terrible-looking devils or demons at the field near the river where we had our swim and washed our clothes. Those devils or demons would leave him only when we called on the name of Jesus.

Our mother could no longer cope with the problem by herself. On my part I did my best, but then I did not know what to do when the seizure happened. All I could do was to pray silently with my mother when our father was not there. Then I would help to hold his mouth because he would always try to bite or hurt his own tongue.

When the frequency and the seriousness of his seizure became more and more, our father had to resign from his job as a mission morning school teacher at Ageville. He had to be home twenty-four-seven and when our father was there; the frequency was much less than when he was not there. It appeared as if these devils or demons were afraid of our father.

We tried all the ways and means to cure this dreaded disease. At first, we consulted the allopathic doctors who gave the medicines. However, these medicines had no effect at all.

We never knew at what time this seizure would come. Sometimes, when we were having food, sometimes when we were praying. Sometimes my brother would ask for pocket money and when our mother refused, he would have the seizure.

He would never have the seizure when he was happy. But once he became unhappy or sad, automatically, the epileptic seizure would definitely occur. Our parents tried to make him happy, but how long can you make a boy happy?

His demand became more and more unreasonable. Therefore, sometimes our parents would refuse his demands and this would make him suffer from epileptic seizure. Many times, his demands were so stupid and unreasonable that it was impossible for us to give in to his demands.

The next problem was his schooling. At school, if any of his schoolmates quarrelled with him, he would have an epileptic seizure. Somebody from school would come running to me to tell me about this problem. Other times, when the teacher was not happy about his homework or answers, he would have a seizure.

At other times, out of the blue, he would have the seizure. This would create an uproar in the class and the school. As a result, the school advised our parents to keep him at home until he recovered completely from the dreadful illness.

The other problem was the cordial atmosphere and peace at home. Our family was the best and an ideal family one could say. Our parents were honest and hard-working and therefore we were not rich, but much better than many others.

Another problem was our economic condition. We were not rich but were well off by the standard of the community. Our father was a mission school teacher and hard working. Our mother was the equivalent of Proverbs 31:10–31, ". . . Many women have done excellently, but you surpassed them all. . ."

However, this dreaded disease had taken a toll on our income and savings. We spent all the money we had on medicines and his treatment. Whenever our parents came to know that some doctor or quack who could cure this kind of problem, they would go there to get the treatment to cure my brother.

The problem was not only the expenses for his treatment but the time they spent. They have to neglect many productive works to care for him and search for his cure from near and far. This had a tremendous effect on our economic condition and we were almost broke.

There were many other problems, but the most important was the test of faith. The first problem was our family prayer. If my brother did not want to pray, and if we forced ourselves to pray, he would definitely have a seizure.

Then the more serious problem was that our parents, out of desperation and love for their son, would almost go to any length to get the magic cure for their beloved son. Their desperation and love for their son, without knowing, they neglected me, their other healthy son.

Many acquaintances would inform our parents that there were experts and diviners who could cure these types of disease. As the allopathic medicines did not help, our parents, despite their apprehension, would try out.

These diviners and traditional healers, when they came to know about the problems, they told our parents that the boy was demon possessed and needed to make animal sacrifices to cure him. When our parents refused, these traditional healers and diviners told our parents that if you love your son, to do as you were told. They told our parents that there was no cure for this type of illness except making animal sacrifices to make these devils and demons happy and leave.

But our parents have unflinching faith in God and the blood of Jesus to heal. Therefore, they would never succumb to making animal sacrifices. When we discussed this at home, our father would tell us that making those sacrifices would never end.

Those devils and demons would keep on asking things from us. The arguments would always end with a quote, ". . .*your faith has made you well. . .*" from what Jesus always said in the Bible. They have faith in the healing power of the blood of Jesus and that was that.

Why did my brother have to suffer his first epileptic seizure when our father was praying? Can our parents win this extraordinary battle to test their patience and their Christian faith? Can this unflinching faith cure my brother?

3

Who Were Those Snakes?

WHEN THE GRASSES SWAY, *there's the breeze blowing. Are we able to understand those deep, subtle signs coming into our lives?*

It took me a very long, long time, almost a lifetime, to realise who those three snakes were, for these were forewarnings or signs to us. I kept searching for answers about who would be the most likely candidates?

Then one night recently, I was lying awake and could not sleep. I was thinking about who could be these snakes we encountered while walking with my father? Then suddenly, the answer was as clear as the sun shining brightly.

Before my younger brother suffered from epileptic and demons possessed seizures, we studied at the same village school. Both of us were doing well in our studies.

During this time, our father faced a dilemma regarding his teaching job at Ageville. First, his salary was a peanut amount of thirty rupees per month. It was not worth even half a dollar at today's rate. The only extra money our father earned was by burning and selling charcoal.

However, in our mother's village, there were better opportunities. The village was a short distance away from the city and had excellent road connectivity. If you were hardworking, there were more possibilities for progress in life here than in Ageville.

We were also growing up. Our father knew the pressures and problems of raising young boys. He did not want to leave that pressure and burden on his wife alone. He wanted to be there with us so that he could oversee our education and provide proper guidance for our future.

Then, my brother suffered from demonic epileptic seizures. When he saw the suffering my brother had to undergo, he took a decision. With a heavy heart, he resigned from his job as a morning mission school teacher at Ageville.

After he left his job, as a son, I looked up to my father to provide me with the necessities of life. But he had other priorities like treatment and medicines for my younger brother. But how long can you ignore the rebellious young teenager?

I worked too hard. I woke up early in the morning before the sun rose. My first duty was to fetch water from the nearby well because keeping milking cows needed a lot of water. Then I would prepare food for the cows.

Then I would milk the cows and later feed them. After finishing all these chores, I could have my breakfast. After breakfast, I had to clean the utensils at home and also the utensils for the cattle.

After that, I would go to people's houses to distribute the milk. I would then come back home to prepare myself for school. In case I made any delay or was late in feeding or milking the cows, I had to take my school bag along while distributing milk. After that I would go straight to school and leave the milk pot at my relative's house near the school.

During lunch break, I would come running home to have my lunch and feed the cows with grasses or hay. Then I would look after the goats we tied with ropes and change their grazing place. After that, I would rush back to school, otherwise I would be late at school and punishment awaited those who were late.

When school was over by around three o'clock in the afternoon, I would rush back home and have my afternoon tea. Then I would have to go cutting grass to feed the cows. At other times, I would have to go to the bigger forest on the other side of the village for fire-woods. There had to be enough grasses or hay for the cows and enough fire-woods to prepare food for the cows and also for home.

On Saturday, we got half-day from school. But then we have to get double or enough grasses or hay to feed the cows on Sunday. We never go cutting grass or collecting fire-woods on Sunday.

However, for milking and distributing milk to people's houses, there was no holiday or Sunday. No rain, wind, snow or sunshine would stop my daily routine or duties twenty-four-seven.

All the earnings from selling milk, I would give to my parents and they would spend the amount on those urgent needs, like food and medicines for my younger brother.

I worked so hard that I have no time for leisure or play. I had no money or savings of my own. On a rare occasion that I could watch a village football match, and so often while my friends were enjoying those things teenagers enjoyed, I had to rush home because it was time to milk or feed the cows.

At the beginning, I did all these with no grudges or complaints. But for how long? My peers and friends did not have to work as hard as me, but they have money, new clothes and new shoes while I got no money but only second-hand clothes or shoes.

I used to go to church with clean clothes because my mother would wash and clean the clothes, but all these were never new but old clothes. When there were bigger church gatherings, I would not go because I did not have new or good enough clothes.

Then how long could you keep the young teenager working like a slave but got nothing, so to say, for returns. Slowly and steadily, frustration set in. Once the frustration got a foothold in my heart, other small devils and demons of life started making my heart their dwelling place.

Once these things of the world got hold of my heart, I saw life differently. Then I saw a problem in everything, especially with my father. I found fault with everything my father did. I first avoided the family prayer because that would trigger the epileptic seizure of my brother.

I would do my duties routinely, but I would not listen to my father because I saw him as the principal cause of the problems in my life. I had to put the blame on someone else rather than the circumstances of life.

Then came the decision that I should have a life of my own. Every night, after I finished my duties, I would leave home and visit my relatives or friends' home. There I would have fun like playing games and other teenager things. I would come home late at night, and then go to sleep avoiding my parents.

There came a point in my life that when my parents, especially my father, would say right that I would turn left. Whenever he would tell me to do this or that, I would intentionally irritate him by doing the opposite.

What was most illogical were the words I used. I simply no longer care what was important to me. Life has no more meaning when everything was a problem. The only good thing I had in my life was when I was away from home enjoying with friends. That too, time went so quick when you have some good times.

Then came the rumours from people that my father practiced witchcraft. It devastated the family and created further tension at home. I knew the rumours were uncalled for, but rumours were rumours. How did it start?

To pray at home was almost impossible because the moment we prayed, my brother would suffer from his epileptic seizure. There was no way to stop my parents from praying. The problems we faced called for more and unceasing prayers. If it was not possible to pray at home, then where do you go to pray?

A forest of pine trees and other small tropical trees surrounded our house on the slope of a beautiful hill. This forest was a perfect place for my father to spend his praying time early at dawn and after dark at night. Almost every day, he would go to this forest to plead with God to cure his disobedient first son, his epileptic second son, and heal the family.

I used to wonder why my father hardly had food at night. When our mother offered him food, he would say he was not hungry. He would have only a cup of tea, or sometimes ginger or black pepper tea, but hardly a normal dinner. Only later in my life, I realised my father was fasting.

In a small village, if you go to the forest daily, early at dawn and at night, to pray, people would surely know about it. Many times, inside the forest, my father would kneel and pray loudly, pleading with God to heal his sons, a disobedient elder son and demons possessed and epileptic younger son.

There were many people who appreciated our father for his devotion, prayer, trust, and faith in God. But there were exceptions, and it was a sad thing that a person went to pray and plead with God, but people who saw that took it otherwise.

Many people in the village were simple folks and God fearing. However, when those few unsympathetic people saw the epileptic seizure of my brother, they blamed it on my father. Therefore, this rumour created unnecessary pressure and embarrassment to me as a young teenager.

Finally, when I was in standard eight, I was at the height of my disobedience. Then one day my parents told me that since I have always disobeyed them and did the opposite to what they told me to do, it was better for me to stop going to school.

That was what I was waiting for, for them to tell me to stop going to school. I have had enough problems in my life that it no longer matter to me whether I continue studying. So, when they told me that, I simply stopped going to school.

One day, my father asked me why I did not go to school. I replied that since you told me to stop going to school, therefore, I just obeyed what you told me. My father, being the wise man, stopped arguing with me because he knew what I would say and do. As of now, nothing would change my mind.

You could now understand the consternation in my parents, especially my father. He had spent all his life teaching me the deeper lessons of life and all that he knew how to teach his son. He had taught me all those important and deep things in life and he had a high expectation from me. Now, his son stopping going to school meant an end to that expectation.

Now it was difficult to accept, but those three snakes we encountered on our path were just signs and indications of what was coming.

The first not-so-big snake was that my father had to resign from the job he loved. He had to take a hard but quick decision to sever the ties because he had to progress in life's journey.

The second big blackish snake we encountered on the journey was just a sign or forewarning that my younger brother would suffer from demons possessed and epileptic seizures.

Then what about the third big greenish snake? What did it signify for? It was difficult to accept the fact, but now I realised that the third snake was none other than me. I had become a thorn in my father's flesh.

But the big question was, can the unflinching faith in God, fasting, prayer, patience, wisdom, and love of my parents overcome these seemingly insurmountable problems of life?

The answer is in the next chapter.

4

The Miraculous Cure

THEY PRAYED WITHOUT CEASING, fasted, and have faith. Then miracles happened.

I knew my father had fasted and prayed at home and in the forest. But what about my mother? Did she fasted and prayed like my father?

Yes, she fasted and prayed like my father, but differently. She prayed while sweeping and cleaning the house. She prayed while working at home and in the field.

Even when she was washing clothes, she prayed. She spent her waking hours praying silently for her first disobedient son and her second demon's possessed epileptic son.

They prayed and asked in faith for years, and shall God answer them? I had my doubts, but my parents kept on praying and asking despite it seeming impossible.

At first I thought God did not hear their prayers because if He heard, He would have done something. I looked at the situations at home and thought it was better to stop praying because it was useless. The situations had turned from bad to worse, from hopelessness to despair.

But God has His own ways and timing. When we were in near total despair and almost at the breaking point that God answered. The miracles my parents seek happened at the time where I thought it was no longer possible.

On the first day I did not go to school, I enjoyed my life thoroughly. After I finished my usual duties and at the time I used to go to school, I went to the nearby forest to roam and enjoyed being alone with nature and a good view of our village.

On the second day, I did the same, but the enjoyment diminished. I roamed the forest and lay down in one place trying to sleep, but sleep won't come. The pine and other trees became too familiar to me. I tried talking to them, but they did not talk back.

On the third day, I did the same. But this time, I saw nothing great in the forest except that I missed my school. I missed my classmates and friends. I missed the laughter and jokes. But most importantly, I missed the teachers and the lessons they taught me.

Every day I would go to the forest surrounding our house to kill time. There I would talk with the wild flowers, the wild shrubs, the pine trees and other tropical trees, telling them my dilemma. I would come home only when it was time to eat or when it was time to do my daily chores.

I did not realize the value of education and the beauty of going to school until I stopped going to school. Many times I cried while I was alone in the forest, but I was too proud to ask forgiveness from my parents.

One day I saw the head teacher from the school came to our house. I fled from home because I did not want to meet him and embarrass myself. I knew the head teacher came searching for me because I was absent from school for almost two weeks.

Later that evening, when I came home, my mother said to me,

"Your head teacher from school came searching for you."

"What did he want?" I asked her.

"He wanted you to go back to school."

"Will you send me back to school? Will the school accept me back when I stop going to school for two weeks?"

"Yes, we wanted you to go back to school. We discussed the matter with your father and he wanted you to continue your studies. I also told the head teacher that you stopped going to school because of our economic conditions.

The school was more than willing to accept you back. All you have to do is write a formal letter and I will sign it. The head teacher told me they will continue to give you the merit scholarship you got since you were in Class VII if you go back to school."

I hugged my mother for a long, long time, cried and asked for forgiveness. That night I wrote the letter to school and my mother signed it. The next day, proud to wear my school uniform once again, I took my school bag and went to school. I handed the letter to the head teacher. He accepted it with a smile.

But most important was the immense happiness it brought to my parents, especially my father. But the most precious thing was that it brought me joy and thrill to go back to school.

Were the two weeks I did not go to school wasted? No. I spent those two fruitful weeks roaming the forest and learning wonderful things from the book of nature. I observed that the tiny insects, the ants, the bees were happy in their life doing the things they did. They never complain.

Same thing with the wild flowers, the shrubs, the pines and other trees. They bear all that came to them. Whatever they have, they show their beauty and make the natural world more enigmatic. For two weeks I did not go to a formal school, but I went to the natural school and learnt many important lessons in life.

When I went back to school, my life changed completely. I tried to be the best son for my parents.

Then what about the sufferings of my brother? He suffered from the demon's possessed epileptic seizures for over three years now, and there was no cure in sight. Will God listen to our prayers and bring miraculous healing?

I was at school when a cousin visited our home. He had married and settled in another village. This cousin, when they discussed the sufferings and illness of my brother, told my mother what to do. Out of desperation, our mother did exactly what this cousin told her.

The next day, she prayed fervently before she went to the river where we had our bath on that fateful day my brother had his first epileptic seizure. As told by the cousin, she took a bucket with her. She went to the river at the exact spot we took our bath.

On reaching the spot, she slowly dipped the bucket and in one sweep collected the water from the river along with sands and pebbles, whatever came into the bucket. About three-fourths of the bucket was water, while the rest was sand and pebbles.

She came home and transferred the whole contents to a large pot, boiling it until it reached a full boil. Now she mixed this mixture of water, sands, and pebbles with clean water and left it for some time to let the sands settle down and the water clear enough to bathe.

My brother was over fourteen years old, but this cousin told my mother to bathe him by herself. My mother bathed and washed my brother thoroughly with this water, careful enough not to disturb the sands so that the water was clear enough to bathe.

This cousin told our mother not to use all the water but to leave a small portion of it, especially the sands and pebbles.

After a thorough bath with this water, she poured it back into the bucket with all its contents of sands and pebbles. With this bucket in her hands, she walked the village path back to the river with silent prayer to God to give her the strength and wisdom to do what our cousin told her.

On reaching the river, with all her heart she poured out and shouted these words:

"God created this river and its water for use by humans. My husband and my sons came here to take a bath and washed their clothes. That was the purpose God created the waters and rivers and many other things for use by human beings.

Since God created this river and water, He gives us humans the right to use it. Since it is our inalienable rights to use the river and its water, you, the devils and demons, have no right whatsoever to enter and torture my son, Arnus."

The cousin had told her to use the proper name. Now, she threw all the contents from the buckets into the river and shouted again,

"My husband and my sons had used this water as intended by God. Now I am throwing this water back into the river."

With this, she emptied the bucket and washed it clean and said again,

"These contents are now thrown into the river. The river will carry away all the contents that were thrown into it, as well as all the pains and sufferings of my son, Arnus. As the water once flowed cannot come back, so also the pain and sufferings of my son will never come back.

I declare from this time onwards, no devils and demons will enter to possess my son, Arnus. I declare my son, Arnus, cured and freed from demons and devils in the name of God the Father, Jesus Christ our Lord and Savior, the Son and the Holy Spirit. Amen."

She came back home carrying an empty bucket, but full of prayer and hope. That was almost fifty years ago and to this day, my brother remains fully cured of this dreaded disease.

Back then, I took this cure as a miracle and an answer God gave to my parents for their fasting, prayers and faith. Later in life, I kept on thinking about this miraculous cure. There were questions I wanted answered.

One day, about two years back, I went to visit this cousin who was now in his eighties. I asked him many questions and found him very sharp and his memories have shown no sign of decline.

Then I took out my mobile phone and asked him if I could record our conversations because I needed to know the truth. He gladly accepted my request and told me to record everything.

"Please tell me how and why you visited our home when my brother was suffering from demonic epileptic seizures."

"I knew your brother was suffering from this terrible disease. I thought of visiting your home but kept putting off until that day. There was a small silent voice or a kind of nagging in my heart to visit your house.

When I reached there, only your mother was home. We discussed many things and especially the sufferings of your brother. She told me how you, your father and brother went to the river to bathe and wash and later that night your brother had his first demonic epileptic seizure.

While she told me the entire story, she cried. I took your mother as my mother and when I saw her cry, silvery tears flowed from her eyes, it pierced my heart and also made me cry.

After stopping crying, your mother said, now I don't know what to do. When she finished speaking, I felt lost and unsure of what actions to take; I believed there had to be a solution. Then deep in my heart, a small silent voice told me to tell her what she should do. . ."

He told the exact things he told our mother almost fifty years ago, which she did exactly as he told her.

"From where did you get this knowledge or wisdom to tell our mother what to do?" I asked him.

He replied, "No, I had no special knowledge or wisdom. The angelic face of your mother convinced me that's what she should do. I had never said or done this before and I have never said or done it later in my life. I am extremely happy that it worked.

Now that you asked me, I am convinced it was the nudge and voice of God. I firmly believed that God answered the prayers your parents asked for years. I am not a sinless man, but God used me to carry the message to cure your brother. Your brother's cure is a miracle because nothing is impossible with God."

Well, God answered the prayers of my parents and miraculously cured me, and especially my brother.

5

The Scars

You may doubt what I said, but I can show you the scars.

Those two weeks I did not attend school, but roaming the forest near our home was the most needed break I took. Those two weeks taught me many important lessons and changed my life.

The rain may destroy the anthill, but the ants would not stop rebuilding it. The bees never knew when someone would take away the honey they made, but they continued collection of honey from the flowers.

Well, I can keep on complaining because life is difficult. Perhaps I looked and concentrated only on those problems, which everybody had, but not on the good things in life which there are many.

In the impenetrable silence and the beautiful sound of the forest, I cried out,

"God, I look at my life and see only problems. I had stopped going to school thinking I would be happy, but I found no peace. Now I want to go back to school. Please give me the power to understand and accept the things in my life as they are. Please help me."

I heard only the deafening silence of the forest as no one answered my prayer. I never knew how God would answer my prayer. Despite the circumstances, I found joy in being able to call upon God.

Well, I was stunned when I came back home that day and my mother told me that the head teacher came searching and wanted me to go back to school. I was stunned when my parents sent me back to school because they accepted me and my disobedience as part of my growing up.

That night while lying in my bed thinking, I found out and learnt that acceptance was the key. Pointing fingers and putting the blame on others would only bring miseries.

The bugs, the bees, the birds and others accepted what they got and did their best. My parents accepted me despite what I did to them.

Once I refused to blame others but accepted my fate and circumstances, I found the burden of my soul and hard work became much lighter. Before my acceptance, I saw a problem in almost everything, but now I saw these as part of life and a chance for me to do better, rise above those problems, and to progress in life.

Could I rise above those problems and progress forward in life? My life was full of surprises and lessons to learn, and here are a few of them.

After school one evening, I headed to the large forest across our village to cut grasses. I had a big bamboo basket, called *polo*, used for carrying grasses and other items. With me, I had a sharp sickle in my hand for cutting grasses. I ventured into the deeper side of the forest to get quality grasses for our cows.

On reaching the place where there were quality grasses, I started cutting with the sharp sickle. I was in a hurry to fill the bamboo basket, because I did not want to be in the forest after dark. I cut the grass a little quicker than normal, enjoying the gentle breeze and being alone.

In my hurry to cut the grasses, I tried to cut one portion of grasses where there was also a small shrub. With my left hand, I hold the grasses while with my right hand I pull the sickle to cut these grasses from below. When I pulled the sickle with force, it passed through the small shrub and cut my left thumb.

Because of the force I used, the sickle had cut and almost split my thumb into two halves. The pain was intense that it felt almost unbearable that with a loud voice, I cried,

"WOW, please, help me!"

I threw the sickle and looked at my thumb. The cut was so severe that my thumb was almost in two separate pieces, and bleeding. The pain was excruciating, but I was alone in the deep forest.

I sat down and did not know what to do. Alone in the large forest and with no one around, but despite my uncertainty of how God would intervene, I prayed a silent prayer.

While sitting there alone, I somehow hold the base of the thumb with my right hand to stop the flow of blood and to ease the pain. The agony was so unbearable that tears flowed down my face.

I heard the rustle of leaves and there appeared a complete stranger. This stranger was also cutting grasses on the other side of the forest. When he heard my shriek, he knew something was wrong and came to investigate.

This stranger was from a different community. They spoke a language that was not like ours. He could not speak my language and I cannot speak his.

Because of our inability to talk to each other, we resorted to sign language. I showed him my thumb, and he understood. There was a look of concern on his face, but what could he do to help me?

Then this stranger did the unthinkable. He turned away from me and took off his not-so-clean lungi, a kind of dhoti or a cloth he wore around his waist. With his sickle, he cut this lungi and made one long strip of cloth. With this strip of cloth, he wrapped it around my wounded thumb.

He did this with such care and gentleness that it amazed me. Here was a stranger whom we could not talk with words but took care of me with love. Not only that, but he did one more unthinkable good deed. He collected the grasses I had cut and put those inside my bamboo basket.

As the basket was not yet full, he cut some more grasses until it filled up. I just looked at this stranger with amazement. When the basket was full, he motioned for me to take and carry it. He signalled to me to follow him. I followed him to the place where he kept his grass.

He signalled to me not to go home alone but to wait for him because it was almost dark and he was concerned about the wound and my safety. Instead of using a bamboo basket like me, he used a large jute sack to put his grasses.

When his sack was full, he carried his own portion of grasses while I followed him, carrying my basket full of grasses. From there, we came and walked together up to a point near my village and then we parted because now he knew I would reach home.

The amazing thing was that this stranger did all this with love and compassion. We accomplished all this without saying a single word. The strip of white dhoti cloth around my thumb had become brownish-red because the bleeding had seeped into the cloth, but the pain had subsided and bearable now.

The wound took weeks to heal. But the scar is still there with me till this very day. Here's another similar incident.

After my brother was fully cured from the demonic epileptic seizures, he took over the milking duties at night. This enabled me to work for an extra job to help earn extra money for the family.

My cousin's husband owned a furniture making shop, and I worked part time as an apprentice there. I worked in this furniture making shop whenever I got free time, from 10.00 AM until they close, at 10.00 PM

They paid me one rupee per hour, and the total wage depended on the number of hours I worked. The wage I got was tiny indeed, but at the end of the week, it was good enough for us to buy the things we needed at home.

Then one night while I was working making a rectangle hole for a door frame, I hit the chisel. I did not know how, but the chisel slipped and instead of hitting the wood, it hit and pierced deep in my thigh. The pain went to my brain, and I screamed in extreme pain.

My fellow worker pulled out the chisel from my thigh, and blood started oozing from the wound. The chisel had pierced through my old pants I wore and made a deep gaping wound.

When he saw the bleeding, my cousin's husband, the owner of the furniture shop, took out his homemade polishing mixture and with this mixture, he poured into the wound to stop the bleeding.

This mixture had brought extra pain, and I screamed in agony. The pain was unbearable, and I danced around screaming. I was angry with my cousin's husband for pouring the mixture and making the pain more.

But then, after a few minutes, the bleeding stopped as this mixture deaden the skin and the flesh. The pain was now bearable.

The wound had healed, but the scar is still there in my left thigh up to this day.

From these incidents, I learned many things and important lessons in life. These are just some of them:

When I stopped going to school, I got the freedom I wanted and I could do whatever I wanted to do. But that freedom did not bring me joy and happiness as I had thought. I missed those classes in Maths, Algebra, English and many other things. But most importantly, I missed the learning process at school. Funny, I did not want to go to school, but now I want to go back to school. I realised I did not value education so much until I stopped going to school.

Those experiences in the forest were good but won't carry me to another world of higher learning as a school. If I have to progress in life, I have to get a proper education and then only can I achieve better things in life.

Problems of life are unavoidable, but I don't have to get stuck in those problems. Do something or change the course of your life or get out of those problems as soon as possible. As my father had taught, when you are in the wilderness of life, climb higher, do not get stuck below.

Then I learned that putting the blame on others increased the problems, but once I accepted my fate and my life, hard work became a fascination. I learned from my parents and nature that hard work is essential for accomplishing anything worthwhile in life.

I was alone in the forest when I hurt myself. But when I needed help, I shouted and prayed. Somebody heard my shouts and came to help me. That stranger, without a single word uttered, gave me the best he could. It was the same in the forest of life as there's always somebody out there to help me if I asked.

Many times we look and made friends with people based on the colour of their skin, their language, education, status, etcetera but I have learned that in the forest of life, all I needed is a fellow human beings who out of compassion and love, would take out his clothes, bind my wounds and help me in times of needs.

I did not see the stranger, because the trees and other things blocked my view of him, but he heard my cries. Same thing, I could not see God with my human eyes, but He is always there and hears my cries. He binds my wounds with care, compassion, and love.

My cousin's husband poured into my wound with the polish mixture that increased the pain many folds. He did this not because he hated me, but because he cared for me. That mixture deadened the flesh and skin and stopped the bleeding and quickly healed the wound.

Many times, I thought the Lord added more salt to my pains. From one minor pain created by my silly mistake, to the next greater pain, and many times, it seemed unbearable to me. Only later and after healing did I learn He did this out of love and compassion and by applying the right mixture, even though it increased the pain, it healed the wounds quicker.

Another lesson was that we can create beautiful things. Skilled carpenters could transform those shapeless woods of planks and timbers into beautiful furniture like chairs, tables, and many other useful things. Life is also wonderful because we can create beautiful things in life with hard work.

Last but not the least, I am also like those shapeless woods of planks and timbers where God the Maker twisted, turned, cut, and chiselled to make me useful. After that, He applied that polish mixture to make this little piece of furniture shiny, useful, and beautiful.

6

The Strange Case of an Iron Thread

SOMEONE DISCARDED THOSE TINY useless things. For some other and on certain occasions, those tiny discarded things became absolutely necessary to move on in life.

The teachers, because of my hard work and dedication, expected me to pass my matriculation or standard ten examination with an 'A'. But when I got the result, I found out that I passed with a 'B'.

While my parents were happy with my achievement, I couldn't help but feel disappointed. The hard work I have to do has taken a toll on my overall studies. Anyway, I had to accept the result as the saying goes; you reaped what you sowed.

Then came the problem of my higher studies. By this time, my father had again started his new teaching job at another remote village and also worked as a missionary worker for a cluster of villages. His salary was one hundred rupees per month which was peanuts if you consider the cost of living. Therefore, with this income, it was impossible for me to study in a day class at a day's college.

All the hard work and especially the suffering of my brother from demoniac epilepsy, despite being cured now, had taken a toll on our mother's frail health. This had also taken a toll on our income and economic conditions.

To enable me to continue my studies, my younger brother chipped in by working as a cowherd with our uncle. But the overall cost, I would have to earn by myself.

When we counted the cost, it was impossible for me to study full time in a college for a course we called Pre-University in those days or class eleven today. Therefore, there was no other way for me but to pursue my studies in Arts subjects at night in the nearest college in the city, to enable me to work during the day to support myself.

It was exciting for me to study in a college. There were many interesting stories about my study there and this is one of them:

One evening, I walked from my house and along the road, waiting for a bus to go to college. While I was walking, somehow I found lying on the road, one small piece of an iron thread measuring about a foot long.

I absentmindedly grabbed this small iron thread and started fiddling with it. While I was fiddling with this small iron thread, the bus came and I got on the bus. I sat inside the bus and totally forgot about the iron thread.

I reached the college on time. The night classes started at five o'clock and were over by eight o'clock at night. As I am interested in history, I took it as one of my subjects to study. However, the subject of history was always at the end of the classes and therefore I had to stay till eight o'clock. Sometimes, the professor would take longer to wind up the class and therefore, I would be late coming out.

Tonight, the professor took extra time to go over the subject, causing class to finish at eight fifteen. Then it took about another fifteen minutes to walk from the college to the bus station. I reached the bus station after over eight thirty.

To my surprise, I found all the buses going towards our village had left. There were taxis going to our place, but I did not have enough money for taxi fares. I had enough money only for a bus fare. All my known friends, because they have money, had left by taxis, and I was alone at the bus station.

When it was too late for me to stand and remain alone at the bus station, I left the place and went to another junction waiting for any vehicle for hitchhiking. By the time I reached this junction, it was almost ten o'clock at night.

You can imagine my dilemma. I was alone at night in the middle of nowhere waiting for hitchhike. To say I was afraid was an understatement. I had none to protect me on this stretch of lonely road, except God.

I stood there on the lonely road alone, afraid and nobody to help me. In such circumstances, my only protection was from God. I prayed a silent prayer, asking God to guide me, protect me and lead me home safely.

There were a few vehicles but none would stop when I raised my hands to stop them. Probably, some of them were also afraid of me. What explanation is there for someone being alone on a desolate road late at night?

Then I thought of walking back home. But that option was more dangerous than waiting for hitch hiking. If I walk home, it would take me around two hours to reach home. Then I would have to walk along the lonely road and some stretches of path along forested areas where there was no guarantee of my safety.

After weighing options, I decided that waiting for hitch hiking was much safer than walking alone. I prayed a silent prayer and knew God would never leave me or forsake me in such circumstances.

By around eleven, when all hope of getting hitch hiking was gone, there came one old truck. This truck was a condemned military truck. In those days, the military sold out those condemned trucks to the public.

Some garage or mechanics would refurbish these trucks. After refurbishing these trucks, they would use them for carrying logs or timbers from far away forests where there were not even proper roads.

When I saw this old refurbished military truck came, I raised my hand, signalling the driver to stop and help me. To my surprise, this old condemned but refurbished military truck stopped a little distance ahead of me.

Probably, the driver had a second thought. He might have thought of not stopping, but probably something told him to stop and gave me a lift. When I saw the truck stopped, I ran with excitement and prayer and climbed on the back of the truck.

I stood there alone on the back of the truck, making a small prayer for God to protect me. When the driver knew I was safe at the back of his truck, he drove away.

While climbing the back of the truck, I looked and saw there were about four people, including the driver, all men, inside the truck. They sat along with the driver while I was alone at the back of this truck.

Then a thought came to me. What if these men were wicked men? What if they would do something bad to me? Could I fight them bare-handed? If these were wicked men, there was no way for me to fight against them, but I knew God would fight and protect me.

While I was thinking like this, a strange thing happened. The winding road sloped upwards gradually once we crossed the bridge. While climbing this upward road, the old truck started giving problems.

I knew nothing about the working of vehicles or trucks, but I knew when there was a problem. However, sitting alone at the back of the truck, doubts started cropping in about the problems of this old refurbished truck. Probably, these people were evil men and they intentionally made problems for the truck so that they could do something bad to me.

I stood there alone at the back of this old truck with these doubts. There I told myself, if these people tried something, I would run for my life because there was no way for me, a skinny youth, to fight against four full bodied muscled men.

At one point, the old truck stopped and would not start again. These people tried all they could to make the old truck start and move again. I just stood alone at the back of the old truck, observing what these people were trying to do.

From their body language and what they spoke to each other, I understood that the old truck was having a problem. They were trying to fix the problem the best they could. The old truck moved a little distance, but then it stopped again.

The old truck moved a little distance after fixing the problem, but then it stopped. This happened again and again. From my vantage point of observance, I knew in my heart, the old truck was having a real problem.

It was around midnight when we reached a certain point in the middle of a large forest, where the old truck refused to move. These four people got down from the truck, trying to fix the problem, but they could not. Nothing would make the old truck start again.

Then came the realization that these people were good people. They gave me a lift when I needed one. The old truck gave them a problem, but they tried their best to make the old truck move again. If they were wicked, they would have done something bad, but they did not.

This gave me courage to get down from the back of the truck and went to the front looking for the problem they had. Then I saw they were fixing the rubber pipe connecting with the carburettor. They couldn't fix this rubber pipe properly because they used a strip of cloth for the binding.

Then I put my right hand in my trouser pocket and found that piece of iron thread I collected while walking and waiting for the bus in the evening. I took out this small piece of iron thread I had folded and showed it to them.

It was then that the driver took it from me and shouted with joy,

"This is what we needed most. We could not fix this pipe with the carburettor with a piece of cloth. With this iron thread, we can fix it properly and tightly."

With this piece of iron thread, the driver bound the rubber pipe with the carburettor tightly.

Then the driver climbed inside the old truck and started it. To my surprise, the truck roared and there was no more problem.

I was about to climb to the back side of the old truck when these people did not allow me. They forced me to sit with them inside the old truck, along with the driver. They thanked me profusely.

After getting into the old truck, they asked me about how I came to possess this piece of iron thread. I told them everything. They all laughed at the silly story of me picking up this iron thread and forgot all about it until that time when I gave it to them.

However, one older man said these profound words, "Brother, I think God put that small piece of iron thread for you to pick it up. We thought we would not give you a lift, but the driver thought otherwise. He pitied you and stopped the truck.

We should thank God and you for the iron thread. Because without it, we would have got stuck on the road and with the problem we had, there's no way for us all to reach home tonight."

It was well past midnight when I reach the point where it was near home. The driver stopped the old truck when I asked him. Before I got down, I took out the money I had and offered the driver to pay for the lift he gave me.

But he would have none of it. The iron thread was, to him, more valuable than money. All inside the truck thanked me for the iron thread and I thanked them for giving me a lift.

On reaching home, I found my mother sitting near the fireplace waiting for me. When she asked me why I was so late, I told her everything. Then I asked her why she stayed up so late.

She replied,

"I did nothing but pray for you. God answered my prayer."

I felt elated and fortunate to have a mother who prayed because I believe everything happens for a reason.

Before I fell asleep that night, I realised that those seemingly useless things in life became absolutely necessary in a certain episode of life. Then those people I knew left me alone, but those people I doubted helped me unconditionally.

Our lives are also like that small iron thread. To some, life is useless, but to others, this life can bind things fallen apart and make the broken engine come to life. Then only the refurbished truck of life can reach its destination.

7

United Even in Death

Death separates them. But *death also unites them.*

There were only three of us at home because our father, for the fourth time, had gone and worked as a teacher. He worked as a morning mission school teacher in one village and also served as a missionary worker for a cluster of distant villages.

Because these villages were quite far and accessible only on foot, none of us had ever visited this place. Because you have to walk for hours before reaching the nearest road, our father came home only once in a while.

Tonight, after completing dinner and household tasks, my brother and our mother sat around the fireplace to have meaningful conversations before ending the day with Bible reading, prayer, and sleep.

Our discussion revolved around multiple subjects, such as my college studies, but the future of my brother was the most crucial. Despite being cured of demonic epileptic seizures, he experienced other health issues caused by tapeworms and kidney stones.

Therefore, he had to give up attending school. Later, he worked as a cowherd with our uncle to get extra income and to support my college studies.

While we were discussing these issues, suddenly our mother, as if from another world, spoke these deep and mysterious words,

"My sons, I wish you both were married and that I could see both my daughters-in-law."

We couldn't believe why our mother would say something like that.

"Mother, why do you speak like that? We are too young to get married," we said.

"I know, sons, you are too young," she said, "but deep in my heart, I felt a desire to see both of you married. I just want to see both of you have good wives and settle down in life before I leave this world."

These words were like a sharp knife to us. We hugged our mother and told her not to say such words. We explained to her we were too young to get married; I was just over twenty, while my brother was over seventeen.

Our mother replied,

"Life is uncertain. I never know when God will take me away from you. Because when he does, I would then know both of you had settled down, married and had good wives."

In the night's silence, the three of us sat around the fireplace in our simple house. We knew our mother was not well because she kept on yawning, but she would not let us go to sleep because she had so many things to say and tell us.

"Dear Son," she said to me, "we have tried with all we had to send you to school. We wanted you at least to be a graduate from college. I have prayed, and I know you will do well in life.

However, I am deeply concerned about your brother. He was frequently ill, which prevented him from going to school."

Then, turning to my brother, she said,

"I bless you and pray that you will also be somebody in life. Despite all your sicknesses and sufferings, you will rise above all and have a blessed life."

Again turning to me, she said,

"Son, look after your brother in all spheres of life. Look after your brother, in sickness or in good health. And before I leave this world, please promise me you'll take care of your brother."

When she said these words, all three of us cried. We hugged our mother tightly and tears kept on flowing as the fire almost died down because we forgot to put forward the fire-woods.

Then four days later, on Thursday, after breakfast, I left for work as usual at the furniture shop. I reached there at around ten o'clock. As usual, I took out the carpentry tools and started my work. At around one o'clock, I left the shop and went home for lunch.

When I reached home, it amazed me that our kitchen garden and all its surrounding areas were spick and span because our mother had cleaned everything. She also washed all our clothes, dried them and wrapped them properly. Everything inside and outside our home was in order.

While having our simple lunch together, I asked her why she did all these things when she was not well. But she replied again that life was uncertain. Therefore, anything I put my hands on, I will give my best.

The lunch that day was simple but tastier than usual. But how could I know that was our last lunch together?

After lunch, I went back to work at the furniture shop. As usual, we worked overtime, and the shop would close by ten o'clock at night. However, at quarter to seven, while we were busy, suddenly my cousin came running, telling me to go home because our mother was unwell.

I tried to put the tools and other things in the proper place before leaving, but my cousin would not let me. He told me that our mother was serious and that I should go home immediately.

While we ran to reach home, my cousin told me that after my brother and mother had dinner, our mother went outside because she felt a congestion in her chest and to breathe fresh air. After some time, when our mother did not come back, my brother went out to look for her.

He found her collapsed and lying on the grass in the frontcourt of our house. My brother tried to take her inside the house, but he could not carry her. He called our neighbors, who came and helped to take her inside our house.

I reach home at around seven o'clock. I found our mother lying in her bed. My Aunt, who was a nurse, was sitting near the bed and took care of our mother. The moment I reached home, I gently hugged my mother and asked her how she was?

She tried to speak, but she could not. She opened her mouth, but that was all she did. I sat beside her and held her hands. My brother was not home because he had left to fetch the doctor from the nearby hospital.

I looked at my mother and saw her peaceful, serene face. She tried to speak, but could only move her lips. Through her lips, she communicated with me with those unspoken words, which only I knew and understood.

"My Dearest son, I am going to another world. I loved you and your brother so much that I did not want to leave you, but as you know, I am prepared to leave and meet my Lord. I have fought the good fight, I have finished the race, I have kept the faith.[1]

1. 2 Tim.4:7

My son, please do not forget my counsels, which I have given to you repeatedly. Most importantly, please remember to serve the Lord. Oh! I saw Jesus and His angels coming to take me home. My dear son, goodbye, we shall meet again in Heaven."

I looked at my mother and found her to look tranquil and angelic. I hold her hands and said,

"Get well soon mother, please get well soon."

Just then, my aunt, a trained nurse, shouted,

"*WoW!! WoW!! WoW!! My sister is no more.*"

The volcano erupted inside my heart, but I did not believe what my aunt said. I thought my mother had fallen asleep and she would wake up soon. I thought they made a mistake, my mother would wake up soon.

Then my brother reached home along with the doctor. The doctor examined our mother and shook his head. Our mother had suffered a heart attack.

Then everybody inside the house erupted in crying. Embracing my brother, we both cried, feeling as though the world has ended for us.

With my own eyes, I saw the last moments and the last breath of my mother's life. In life, she exuded a cool and gentle character, and in her ultimate moments, she departed with the same calm and composed countenance.

I did not remember what exactly our relatives did regarding how to inform our father about our mother's death. Because to me, my world has ended. From both sides of the family, my mother's side and father's side, they did their best to inform our father.

They selected two youths to go to the village our father taught. After walking for hours, they reached the village, but unfortunately, our father was not there.

It was wintertime and a holiday for the school. Our father had gone from one village to another for his mission work duty. The villagers where the school was did not know which village our father was in now. Therefore, these two youths came back home without meeting our father.

Therefore, on the third day after her death, on the fifth of January 1980, both sides of our family had to make a decision whether to wait or bury the body of our mother. My relatives consulted me, but ultimately they decided they could not wait for our father forever. They would take the body of our mother to eternal rest without waiting for our father.

At around two o'clock, they prepared to nail the cover of the coffin. I couldn't find the words to describe my feeling that I would no longer see my mother and that they would bury her mortal remains in a grave.

My brother and I were in the room crying together. But a few minutes just before they nail the coffin's cover, a strange thing happened. Our father suddenly appeared and reached home.

Those who were to nail the coffin cover stopped when they saw our father. Our father took off the coffin cover and hugged the lifeless body of our mother.

My brother and I hugged our father tight because we loved him and cried. Those responsible for sealing the coffin had no choice but to watch as the event unfolded before them.

There were many talks about the strange events surrounding our father's arrival home before we closed the coffin. Our mother's love for our father was so strong that her soul went to inform him about her journey to heaven.

Later, when we asked our father how he knew about our mother's death and came home. He told us the night before he had a strange dream. In this dream, he heard our mother's voices telling him she was leaving for heaven and forcing him to go home.

It appeared our father had a premonition and knew he would no longer see our mother alive because of this dream.

Whatever the case, the relationship and the love for each other made them to be united even in death. We, the children, knew, despite the various marital problems and challenges of life, they love, care and trust each other.

The last words our father said to the lifeless body but living soul of our mother were,

"Go in peace, mother of my children."

Our father hardly cried, but today tears flowed from his eyes. From now onwards, they could no longer talk to each other, pray together, and counsel each other.

They met through the Bible, fell in love at first sight, got married, they went through life pilgrimage together and their souls united even in her death. In love they met, and in love they parted.

We were in grief to have lost our mother to death. But what happened to our father strengthened our faith in God. Because humanly, it would have been impossible for our father to know her death, but God told him through a dream.

We all know our mother is forever gone with the Lord and could no longer speak to us. But deep down in my heart, I hear her beautiful, angelic voice,

"Au revoir, we shall meet again in Heaven."

It's this deep, wonderful voice I heard that enables me to move ahead in life, despite the challenges, because someday I will meet her again.

About the Author

Kit Nongkhlaw graduated from Synod College, Shillong in 1984.

He worked for a few years as a civilian in Defense Department, Government of India.

He joined State Bank of India as a probationary officer in 1987 but took voluntary retirement from Senior Management position in 2013.

Then he worked as Finance Secretary, John Roberts Theological College from 2014 to 2022. He has been a Church Elder since 2005 and is a Sunday school teacher for over thirty five years.

The author can be reached at kit.nongkhlaw@gmail.com